HAND-PRINT
ANIMAL ART

*Library of Congress
Cataloging-in-Publication Data*

Carreiro, Carolyn, 1961-
Hand-print animal art/Carolyn Carreiro.
p. cm. — (A kids can! book)
Includes index.
Summary: Provides directions for creating paintings
of all kinds of birds, wildlife, and sea creatures
using your fingers and hands.

ISBN 1-885593-09-0

1. Finger painting—Juvenile literature. 2. Animals in art–Juvenile literature.
[1. Finger painting. 2. Painting–Technique. 3. Animals in art.] I.Title. II. Series.
ND2490.C37   1997
751.4'9—dc21   96-51923
                         CIP
                         AC

Cover design:
Trezzo-Braren Studio

Interior design:
Joseph Lee Design, Inc., Joseph Lee, A. J. Greenwood

Illustrations, Hand-print art:
Carolyn Carreiro

Illustrations, Activities:
A. J. Greenwood

Printing:
Quebecor, Inc.

WILLIAMSON PUBLISHING CO.
P.O. BOX 185
CHARLOTTE, VERMONT 05445
1-800-234-8791

PRINTED IN CANADA

10 9 8 7 6 5 4 3 2

HAND-PRINT ANIMAL ART

by
Carolyn Carreiro

Williamson Publishing
Charlotte, Vermont

Acknowledgements

After years of sharing art ideas with children, I am thrilled to fulfill a life-long dream and to reach even more children through this book. My children have been so excited and understanding while I've been too busy to play. I thank them and my husband for their enthusiasm and support. I would like to thank Elizabeth Cannon at St. Luke's Preschool in Barrington (RI) for her ideas and encouragement and for the opportunity to work freely with so many children. Thank you also to all my wonderful friends, family, and neighbors, for helping me and my children and for just being there whenever I needed you. To all the teachers in the Bristol (RI) Public School Department, you have been terrific. My children and I are blessed with your dedication and hard work. To Brenda Geramia and everyone at the Rogers Free Library, I extend a pat on the back for all the help and encouragement you have given me and for all you do to encourage children to read and be creative. I would like to thank Jack and Susan Williamson and Jennifer Ingersoll of Williamson Publishing Company, for their guidance, support, and hard work. Thanks, also, to Laura and Sam, Brandon and Aaron, and Joseph and Annie, for your colorful little handprints. Last, my thanks goes out to every child I've had the pleasure to work with and care for. Without children, life would be far less fun.

Dedication

To my children Laura and Sam, whose love fills my heart and whose handprints and fingerprints cover my walls! You're the best.

CONTENTS

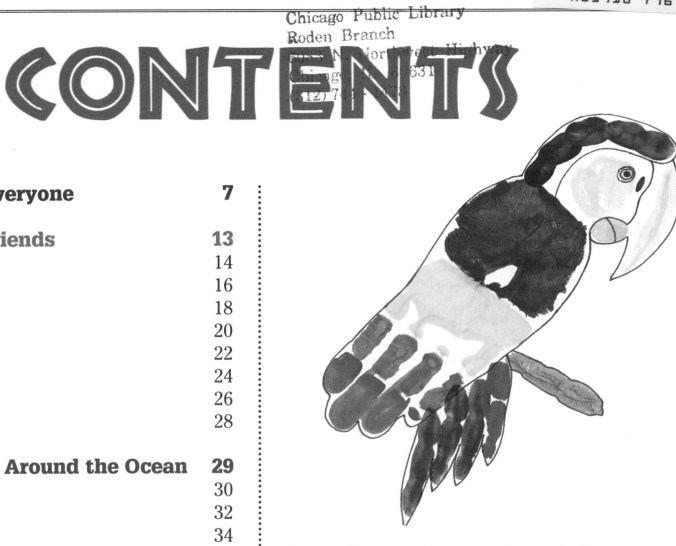

SOMETHING FOR EVERYONE

Express Yourself!

No two handprints are exactly alike, and so, no two works of hand-print art are exactly the same either. By using your hands to make art, you're expressing your individuality as no one else can. Some of the fun of hand-print art certainly comes from painting with fingers, palms, and hands instead of with brushes, but experimenting with different colors and artistic materials and techniques is a lot of the fun, too. All you need to do is press your hands to a piece of paper and something great is bound to happen. Best of all, by using wildlife as the inspiration for your artwork, you're bound to learn a lot about the animals you're creating.

Using Your Hands as Tools

As you paint, think of your fingers, palms, and whole hands as different tools, using them as you would a paintbrush. Avoid moving your hands once in contact with the paper, unless you want to create a vision of movement by smudging your design. With *Hand-Print Animal Art*, following instructions to achieve certain outcomes is important. Using your pinky, for example, instead of just any finger, will create a specific effect, much as a carpenter uses a particular type and size of hammer to achieve a certain end result. Using your hands as unique tools allows you to add a creative dimension to your art. Your hands are different from other people's so naturally your artwork will look different, too. Use varied parts of your hands for special effects. The sides of your hands make interesting jointed lines that you can curve or leave straight, and your palms can make circles or be painted with squares, triangles, and ovals, and then used as a

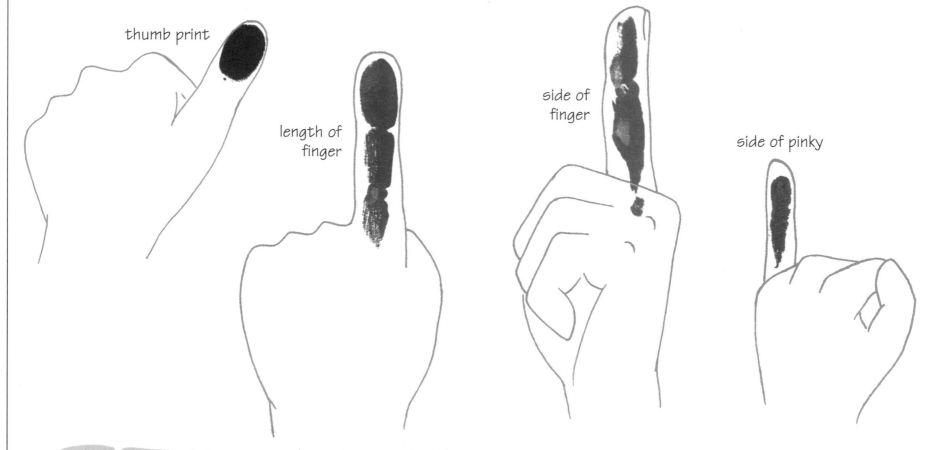

thumb print

length of finger

side of finger

side of pinky

"printing pad." You can even use your palms as a mixing palette for creating new colors — just squeeze a gooey glob of paint on each palm and press together for wild, wonderful colors!

Your fingertips provide a multitude of shapes for your art, varying in size, from your pinky to your thumb — perfect for little eyes or big heads!

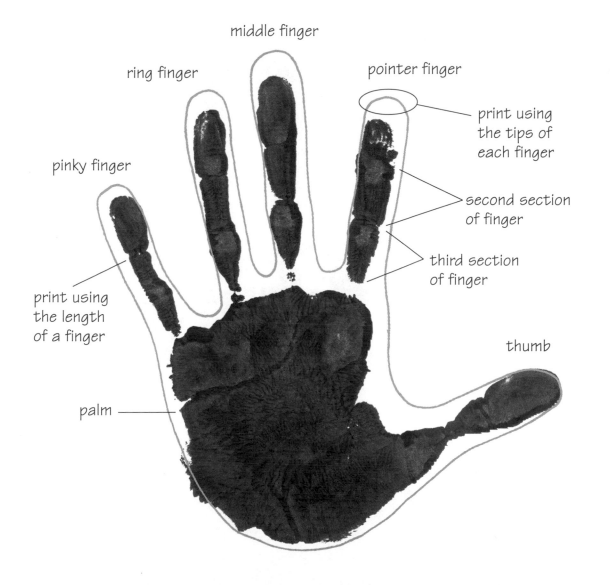

middle finger

ring finger

pointer finger

print using the tips of each finger

second section of finger

pinky finger

third section of finger

print using the length of a finger

thumb

palm

Keys to Confidence

Each hand-print project is marked with one, two, or three fingers, according to its level of challenge. Hand-print art activities with one finger are the easiest of all. Projects with two fingers are a bit more challenging, and those with three fingers are the most challenging and may require many steps or techniques.

 Activities with 1 finger involve 1, 2, and sometimes 3 steps and require only simple hand positioning.

 *Activities with 2 fingers involve more colors and steps to completion. You will still be able to do these prints alone.*

 Activities with 3 fingers include many steps and more complicated hand positioning.

Let's Get Practical

Before you begin handprinting, take a look at the list of colors you'll need for your animal. Some will require bright, vibrant colors, while others will specify browns or grays. Because many animals in the wild rely on camouflage to hide from predators or prey, their fur, feathers, and skin are often colored to blend in with their surroundings. Some projects suggest different options for adding color to less colorful animals. Use them if you wish, or choose any other colors you think will work.

To keep your work area clean, cover it with newspaper and wear an apron, smock, or an old t-shirt with short sleeves when painting. You'll also need a bucket of warm, soapy water and a sponge for rinsing your hands between color changes.

Most projects require dipping your hands in paint, so look for a shallow, flat dish to work from. Washable plastic plates, baking sheets, and Styrofoam trays (from fruits and vegetables only) work great, but anything large enough to dip your hands in will work well as long as it can be cleaned easily. For transferring paint onto certain areas of your hands, you'll need a thick paintbrush. Use sponges to blot off excess paint as you work. Wash the sponges carefully after use with antibacterial soap. Let them air dry for future art fun.

Keeping It Safe

Having a good time sometimes means taking a few safety precautions. When working with paints and glues, always work in a well-ventilated room, or better yet, work outside when possible.

Keep your materials out of reach from toddlers and away from the edge of your work area. And though some activities suggest visiting the ocean, a pond or lake, or a wooded area, never venture to those places without a grown-up.

Wash your sponges, paint trays, and brushes after each session of painting, and avoid using Styrofoam meat trays for paint trays. No matter how well you wash them, they may still contain contaminants.

Colors of All Kinds

When it comes to using color, there aren't any rules — anything goes! Most of the animal print projects list paint colors that reflect each animal's natural color. But you can always try something new and outrageous.

There are several ways to mix up paint colors. Most require using a paintbrush, a clean rag, a plastic container of clean water, and a paper plate.

The colors you choose to use will depend on your mood and on the animal you're creating. When two primary colors (red, yellow, and blue) are mixed, they create secondary colors (green, purple, and orange). Reds and blues make purples, reds and yellows make oranges, and yellows and blues make greens. Similarly, black and white make gray, red and white make pink, and red and green make brown.

Along the way you may want to lighten and darken colors for animals' fur, skin, feathers, and shells. Add a little white to your colors to make them lighter shades or pastels; add a little black to darken colors. By using some yellow with brown, or more red, black, or white, you'll create a whole range of brown shades — from the honey color of a hamster's fur to the deep, chocolate

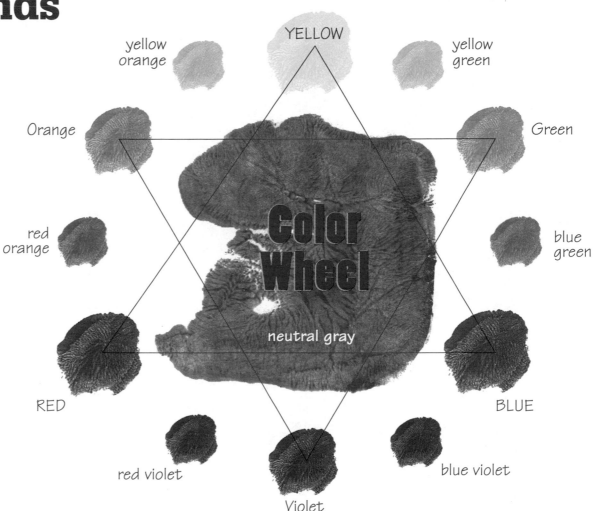

brown of a moose's coat.

Of course, experimental mixing is lots of fun, too. Use a little of this and a little of that to see what colors you come up with. Just remember to rinse your brush between dips. Or, try mixing colors directly on your hands. Put a blob of red on one palm and a blob of yellow on the other; then press them together. Open your hands and behold the fiery orange, red, and yellow swirls you created!

Tips for Texture

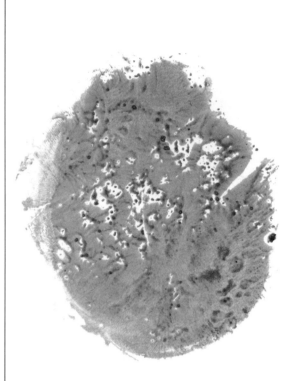

Play around with creating texture to add realistic effects to your paintings. Try different color combinations and patterns on different surfaces like paper or fabric, wood or tile, or rough or smooth paper for textured looks. Experiment as you go and you'll undoubtedly discover a few texture tricks of your own. Here are a few of my own to get you started:

- *Use thick paint for heavy fur and feathers.*
- *Add salt, sand, or eggshells to your paint for a bumpy, scaly look for reptiles.*
- *Add water to paint for smooth skin.*
- *Fingerprint a second color on top of a first color while it's still wet, and watch the colors blend and become "feathery" — perfect for birds or long-haired mammals!*

Good Times Ahead

Hand-print art is about having fun, and just wait till you get started! Along the way, you'll read about some of the funny things animals do. Some facts will fascinate you, others may scare you, and still others may disgust you. But they are all part of the wonderful natural world we live in.

While learning about some animals, you may be surprised by how many species are endangered. There are many organizations today whose sole purpose is to protect these animals and save the places where they live (their habitat). If you're interested in finding out more about these creatures, or you have many questions about them, just take a trip to the library or onto the Internet to answer them (check out the National Geographic Society's website at **www.nationalgeographic.com** or **www.nwf.org** for the National Wildlife Federation's online site).

Let your imagination run wild, just like the animals in *Hand-Print Animal Art*. Use the instructions as a guide, be creative, and it'll be impossible to go wrong. Let the fun begin!

OUR FEATHERED FRIENDS

PARROT

ACTIVITY LEVEL

Mimicking, or copying, what another person says or does is sometimes called "parroting."

What You Need

❥ White paper
❥ Poster paint: red, yellow, green, blue, black, brown, and peach
❥ Fine black marker

What You Do

1 To print the parrot's body, paint your 4 fingertips blue, the second section of your 4 fingers green, and the third section yellow (spreading it onto your palm). Paint the rest of your palm red. Print the body by sloping your hand slightly diagonally so your fingertips face downward and close to the left of the paper.

2 To make the tail feathers, paint the length of your pointer finger red and print 4 times. Repeat with blue paint, printing between the red "feathers."

3 Print the brown perch using the length of your pointer finger.

slight diagonal

4 Print the peach face using your thumbtip print. To print the head, dip your pointer fingertip in red paint and print above the peach face.

Print the beak using the two top side sections of your pointer finger dipped in peach paint. Bend your finger slightly to print.

5 Print the parrot's black chin using your pointer finger.

6 When dry, add eyes and the nostril at the top of the beak, and outline the parrot with marker.

Large parrots have been known to outlive their owners in captivity, reaching the ripe old age of 70 or 80!

Raucous and Intelligent

Parrots are one of the oldest domesticated, or tame, animals in the world and are very popular cage birds. When kept in cages without a parrot companion, parrots will imitate sounds they hear and mimic their human keepers, a trait not seen in the wild. Parrots are loud and raucous, intelligent, and outgoing. Unfortunately, some are becoming rare and endangered.

Inspect a Feather

Feathers play an important role in attracting mates and also in keeping birds warm and dry. Look around your backyard, the beach, or the woods for feathers. Use a magnifying glass to see the barbs on the feather. Pull some apart and listen very closely. Can you hear them "unzip"? Can you see the tiny barbules, or rows of tiny teeth that lock the barbs together like a zip-lock bag? Drop a little water onto the feather. Does the water roll right off or is it absorbed? Why do you think this happens? (See immiscibility on page 111.)

EAGLE

ACTIVITY LEVEL

If someone's ever told you that you have "eagle eyes," that's quite a compliment! Eagles have very good eyesight and can spot a rabbit from the air more than two miles (3 ¹/₄ km) away.

What You Need

❧ White paper
❧ Poster paint: brown, black, white, and yellow
❧ Fine black marker

What You Do

1 To print the eagle's wings, paint both hands brown, leaving your thumb clean. Overlap your palms slightly with your fingers pointed toward the top corners and print.

2 For the legs, dip your pointer fingertip into brown paint and print.

3 Print the white head by painting a small circle on your palm and printing. Print the yellow beak using your pointer fingertip.

4 Print the eyes close to the beak using your pointer fingertip.

5 Print the yellow claws using your pinky fingertip.

6 Outline when dry and add the details to the eyes, beak, and claws.

Making a Comeback

T he bald eagle appears on the National Seal of the United States and is a symbol of power, courage, and immortality. It wasn't long ago, however, that eagles were an endangered species due to pesticide and herbicide use, which weakened eagles' eggs. Fortunately, these regal birds have made a remarkable comeback. Eagles are found the world over except in Antarctica and New Zealand. The eagle's nest, called an aerie, is made high in a tree or on a rocky ledge where it's protected from predatory animals.

Look for Nesting Materials

Depending on the bird, most nests are built with a variety of materials including mud, stones, twigs, leaves, grass, hair, feathers, spiderwebs, snakeskin, and even shells. Some nests are piled, woven or sewn together, or they can be stuck together with the bird's saliva. You can help out your backyard birds with their nest-building by collecting pieces of yarn, lint from the clothes dryer, hair from your hair brushes, even fabric scraps. Place the materials into a mesh bag, the kind you buy onions in, and tie to a tree branch. Watch for visiting birds. Do you notice that some birds like some materials better than others?

COOL COLOR OPTION

Different eagle species have different markings. Some eagles have white and black markings; others have gray, white, and brown markings. You could also print your eagle in gold and make it into an emblem that says something about you.

ROBIN

A robin's cheery song is very easy to recognize. Next time you're outside, listen for the song that sounds like these words: "Wake up, cheer up, cheerily up, wake up!"

What You Need

- White paper
- Poster paint: light and dark brown, white, green, orange/red
- Fine black marker

What You Do

1 To print the robin's light brown body and tail feathers, paint your hand, leaving your thumb clean. Print diagonally with fingers pointing to the lower left corner of the paper.

2 To print the head, dip your palm in light brown paint and print, overlapping the body slightly.

print diagonally ⎯⎯⎯

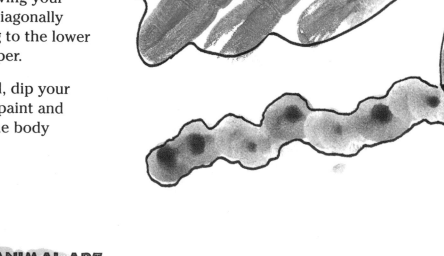

3 Paint the robin's red breast on your palm and print.

4 Print a dark brown beak using the side of the tip of your pointer finger. Print a white eye using your pinky fingertip.

5 To make a wing, paint the length of your pointer finger in dark brown paint and print five times. Print once for each leg.

6 Form the brown branches using pointer fingertip prints. Repeat for the green leaves. Outline the bird and add the claws with a marker.

Naturally Speaking

ONLY 15 DAYS AFTER HATCHING, THE YOUNG ROBIN IS ALMOST FULL-GROWN. IT TAKES HUMAN GIRLS 19 YEARS AND BOYS 21 YEARS TO REACH THEIR ADULT HEIGHTS!

Eye on the Sky

Robins are only one of hundreds of species of birds that head south, or migrate, during the cold winter months. Scientists aren't sure how birds know when it's time to migrate or even how they are able to navigate their way to the same places every year. Robins' arrival to the southern parts of the U.S. symbolize winter's arrival, but to those living in the northern states, their arrival means just the opposite. Robins that make their way to New England, the Midwest, or the Northwest, for example, hold the promise of spring and warm weather.

Keep a Migrating Bird Journal

Watching for the arrival of spring birds is a great way to observe one of nature's incredible mysteries — migration. Visit a nature center, an Audubon center, or use a guidebook to learn about the migratory birds that live in your area. Then, keep a log about the arrival and departure of three different migrating birds. Watch the sky and record the dates you first see them in your neighborhood. Then, in the fall (or spring, in the south), keep track of the last day you see these birds before they leave, or migrate, north or south. Keep track for several seasons and compare arrival and departure dates. Are they about the same every year?

Bird	Arrive	Leave
Robins	March 3	October 15
Canada goose (I saw the geese flying in "V" formation!)	February 17	November 7
Cardinal	December 5	April 10

KIWI

The kiwi is a shy, flightless bird found only in New Zealand. Kiwis are nocturnal birds, which means they sleep during the day and are awake at night.

What You Need

❧ White paper
❧ Poster paint: brown, blue, and yellow
❧ Fine black marker

What You Do

1 To form the kiwi's head, paint a small dark brown circle on your palm and print.

2 To form the body, paint your palm dark brown and print diagonally with your fingers facing the bottom left corner. Overlap the head slightly.

3 Make the eye with a blue fingerprint.

4 Print the kiwi's yellow beak using the length of your pointer finger.

5 Print the brown legs using the length of your pointer finger.

6 Print the light brown feet using the side of your pinky.

7 When dry, add the details to the eye, beak, and feet with a marker. Outline the bird and add the hairs to the top of its head and under its chin.

Sniff Sniff

The kiwi lives alone in humid forests and swamps and uses its long, pointed bill to hunt insects, snails, berries, and its favorite treat — earthworms. A kiwi's bill is quite different from most birds as it has a small nostril near the tip, useful for sniffing out food. That's an unusual trait for a bird!

Eat a Snack — Bird-Style

The kiwi has a bill suited perfectly for hunting and eating certain types of foods. Have you ever noticed the different beak and bill shapes of birds in your neighborhood? Here's a game to play with a friend that will show you just how useful various bird beaks can be. Fill a small bowl with shelled peanuts and raisins. Using an unwound paperclip as the thin, pointed beak of a swallow, collect food from the bowl and place it in front of you. Then, try using a clothespin for a sparrow's thick beak to collect food. Which "beak" collects soft foods like raisins more easily? Which is better for hard, oval-shaped foods like peanuts?

Funny Fact

People who live in New Zealand are often nicknamed "Kiwis."

FLAMINGO

When a young flamingo hatches, its bill is straight, but within a few weeks, the well-known bend begins to develop.

What You Need

❥ White paper
❥ Poster paint: pink and black
❥ Fine black marker

What You Do

1 To form the body and tail feathers, paint your hand pink, leaving your thumb and pinky clean. Print horizontally.

2 Print the head using your thumb. To form the flamingo's legs and neck, use the length of a finger dipped in pink paint.

3 Print the flamingo's black beak and feet using the side of the tip of your pinky.

4 Use your fingertip to print a small black spot for an eye. When dry, outline eye and body with a marker.

A Special Beak

Flamingo feathers can be as light as rosy pink or as dark as vivid scarlet. Try these different colors for several varieties of flamingo.

Wild flamingos once lived in the Everglades of southern Florida; unfortunately, people killed the birds for their beautiful feathers faster than the flamingos could multiply. Today, flamingos live in many parts of the world, but in the U.S., they are found only in zoos and nature preserves.

One of the most unusual traits of a flamingo is how it eats. With its head pointing downward, it feeds by dipping its specialized beak in water, filtering out nutritious water, plants, and tiny animals. The lower bill moves up and down to pump water against the top bill.

Stand on One Leg

Did you ever wonder why flamingos often stand on one leg, switching legs every now and then? Well, because flamingos' legs are long and featherless, they tuck one leg up against their bodies to reduce heat loss from their legs.

While resting, the flamingo balances well on one leg. See how long you can stand on one leg by closing your eyes and having a friend time you with a clock that has a second hand. Usually it's easier for right-handed people to balance on their right leg and for lefties to balance on their left leg. What's easier for you — left or right?

PEACOCK

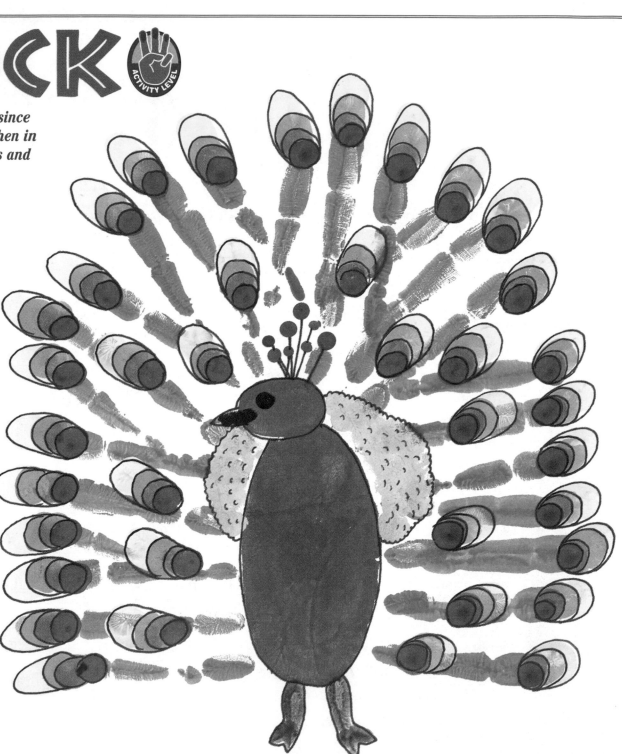

Peacocks and peahens have been kept as pets since the days of Alexander the Great in 336 B.C. When in the wild, peacocks live in open lowland forests and roost in tall trees.

What You Need

▶ White paper
▶ Poster paint: royal blue, dark and light green, black, brown, turquoise, peach, and yellow
▶ Fine black marker

What You Do

1 To print the peacock's body, paint a long, narrow oval of blue paint on your palm; then print toward the bottom center of your paper.

2 For a head looking to the side, dip your thumb in royal blue paint and print.

3 For head feathers, dip your pinky fingertip in royal blue paint and print 9 or 10 times above the peacock's head.

4 To form the peacock's legs, dip the side of your pinky in brown paint and print. Use your pinky fingertip to print the claws.

5 For the feathers, paint your 4 fingers dark green and print all around the peacock several times.

6 For light green tail feathers, use pointer fingertip prints, and print close to the body.

7 To form the black beak, use the side of your pinky fingertip to print. For the eye, use a black pinky tip print.

8 Dip your thumb tip into yellow paint and print at the end of each tail feather. Re-dip your thumb as needed and print a few feathers closer to the peacock's body.

Tip: For the most colorful results, let the paint dry before beginning step 9.

9 Print a peach middle finger print on top of the yellow oval print, a turquoise pointer finger print onto the peach print, and a blue pinky tip print on the turquoise print. Let each layer dry before printing the next.

10 Outline when dry. Add the stems to the head feathers and details to the light green feathers with a marker.

Jewel-Tailed Beauties

The peacock, or male peafowl as it is commonly called, has a magnificent tail of blue, bronze, green, and gold plumage. Many bird species and animals show beautiful coloring in the males, usually to attract females during mating season. The female peahen is brown and lacks the splendid tail and coloration of her mate. She is the one who raises and protects her young. Why do you think being less colorful would be helpful to a mother bird?

Think About It

Watch for different species of birds in your backyard or at the zoo, or look at pictures in bird books. What do you think some of the disadvantages of being brightly colored would be? Would it be easy or hard to attract attention? Would protecting yourself from predators be simple or tough? Would you find it easy or difficult to sneak up on prey?

PELICAN

"A wonderful bird is the pelican;
His bill will hold more than his belican...."
—Dixon L. Merritt

What You Need

❧ White paper
❧ Poster paint: light gray, peach, orange, black, and brown
❧ Fine black marker

What You Do

1 To print the pelican body, paint your palm gray and hold down diagonally with your fingers facing the lower right corner of the paper.

2 Print the head by painting a small gray circle on your palm and overlapping the body slightly as you print.

Funny Fisherman

3 Print the top part of the pelican's peach-colored beak using the length of your pointer finger.

4 Print the pelican's lower beak using the length of your pointer finger and longest finger painted peach.

5 Print the legs and feet using your pointer fingertip dipped in peach paint.

6 Print the black eye and wing feathers using your pointer fingertip; then print the orange area around the eye the same way.

7 Make the ground for the pelican to stand on using small brown fingertip prints.

8 When dry, outline the bird and add claws to the webbed feet with a marker.

P elicans are strong fliers and swimmers. They capture fish and crustaceans by diving into the water from the air or while swimming on the surface. Their huge bills have a deeply expandable skin pouch in the lower part, while the upper half serves as a lid.

Look for pelicans in southern North America where people are fishing. Watch them as they dive headfirst into the ocean to catch their dinner.

Make an Underwater "Magnifying Glass"

Pelicans have great vision and can see fish swimming below the surface of the water. Here's how you can take a look underwater without ever getting wet. Cut the top off a ½ gallon (1.89 L) plastic milk jug, leaving the handle. Cut out the bottom and cover with plastic wrap. Secure the wrap with a rubber band. Ask a grown-up to take you to visit a pond, lake, or slow-moving stream. At the water's edge, press the plastic wrap end into the water until the water comes up the sides of the jug but not into it. Do you notice how the water magnifies, or enlarges, what you see?

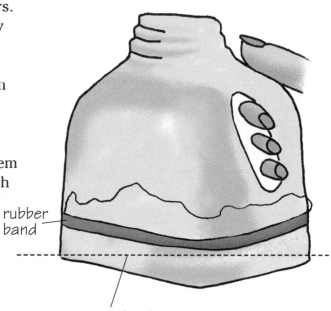

rubber band

water level

PENGUIN

ACTIVITY LEVEL

Some penguins will travel over ice and snow by tobogganing. They pick up speed by using their flippers for that extra push while sliding on their bellies!

What You Need

- White paper
- Poster paint: black, white, orange, and yellow
- Fine black marker

What You Do

1 To make the penguin's body, paint your hand white, leaving your thumb clean, and print in the center of the paper with your fingers pointing upward.

2 To make the head looking to the side, paint a black leaf shape on your palm and print.

3 To form the wings, paint the length of your pointer finger black and print 3 times on each side of the penguin.

4 Make the feet with black fingerprints.

5 Make the yellow feathers around its neck with yellow fingerprints.

6 Make the beak with an orange fingerprint and the eye with a white fingerprint.

7 When dry, outline and add details to the beak and eye with a marker.

Naturally Speaking

A PENGUIN'S WHITE BELLY AND BLACK BACK SIDE CAMOUFLAGE IT WHILE SWIMMING IN THE WATER. FROM BELOW THE SURFACE OF THE WATER, THE PENGUIN'S LIGHT-COLORED BELLY FEATHERS BLEND IN WITH THE SUNLIGHT; FROM THE SKY, THE BLACK BACK FEATHERS APPEAR TO BLEND IN WITH THE DARK OCEAN WATER.

CREATURES IN AND AROUND THE OCEAN

STARFISH

Sometimes called sea stars, starfish usually have five arms, but some can have up to twenty! A starfish's arms are equipped with rows of tube feet or suction cups radiating outward along them.

What You Need

- White paper
- Poster paint: red, yellow, orange, and brown
- Fine black marker

What You Do

1 Print the middle of your starfish in the center of the paper using your thumb dipped in red paint.

2 To print the starfish's 5 arms, dip your longest finger in red paint and print 5 times.

3 Make a sandy background for your starfish using your pointer finger and yellow, brown, and orange paint.

4 When dry, outline with marker.

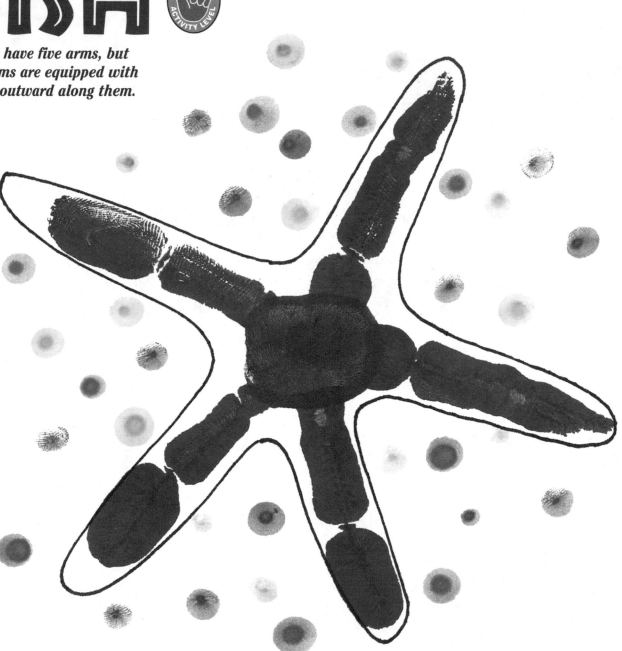

Nature's Folly

For years, fishermen considered starfish annoying, often catching them in their fishing nets. To keep from recatching them, the stars were cut in half and tossed overboard. Much to the fishermens' dismay, it was later discovered that the overpopulation of starfish was due to the regeneration of each half starfish tossed over the deck!

Explore a Tide Pool

Take a look in a tide pool if you get the chance and see what the tide dragged in. Shade the sun by leaning over the pool and peering into the water or use an underwater magnifier (see page 27). Do you see a starfish missing an arm? You may find other marine life like crabs, tiny fish, or jelly fish (don't touch, as some jellies can sting). If you find a starfish washed up on the shore, take it to a tide pool or back to the ocean or it may dry up and die in the bright sunlight. Always be careful when visiting tide pools as seaweed can be very slippery, and always wear shoes while exploring.

Naturally Speaking

SOMETIMES, IF CAUGHT, STARFISH WILL LOSE AN ARM TO AVOID BEING EATEN. LUCKILY, LIKE FIDDLER CRABS AND SOME LIZARDS, STARFISH CAN GROW, OR REGENERATE, AN ARM IF THEY LOSE ONE. EVEN IF A STARFISH IS BITTEN IN HALF, EACH SECTION MAY REGENERATE INTO TWO SEPARATE STARFISH.

CRAB

The blue crab is the most popular crab eaten in eastern North America. After blue crabs molt, or shed their skins, and before a new shell hardens, they're sold and eaten as soft-shelled crabs. Delicious!

What You Need

- White paper
- Poster paint: orange/red and black
- Fine black marker

What You Do

1 To make the crab's body, paint your palm and print onto the paper.

2 Print the crab's legs using the length of your pointer finger.

3 Fingerprint the end of each leg. Print the claws using 2 fingerprints at the ends of the 2 front legs.

4 For eyes, fingerprint 2 black dots.

5 When dry, circle the crab's eyes with marker.

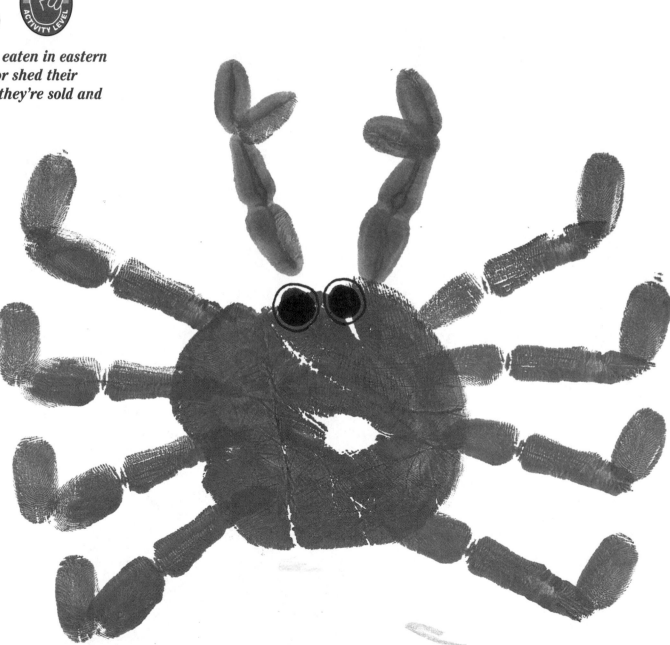

Gimme Shelter

Crabs are found in oceans, fresh water, and even on land all over the world. As crabs grow, they shed their hard shells and grow new ones. Most crabs dig holes or inhabit burrows, but some crabs are creative homebuilders. Hermit crabs, for instance, have a habit of wearing the abandoned shells of other creatures, often decorating them with sponges. The lybia crab, which lives on the sandy bottom of the Indian and Pacific oceans, carries a sea anemone in its claws and uses it to kill or stun its prey. Yikes!

Visit a Salt Marsh

Look for ghost crabs busily running into sand dune holes, fiddler crabs scurrying in salt marshes, or horseshoe crabs wandering a sandy beach. While looking for crabs, keep your eyes open for shells

and unusual rocks on the beach to collect. It's a good idea to disinfect rocks and shells before using them for decoration. Just ask a grown-up to boil the shells or rocks in water for you; then soak them in water with $^1/_4$ cup (50 ml) bleach. Let dry before placing in the bathroom or on a shelf in your home.

Funny Fact

Have you ever heard of the tree-climbing robber crab? It climbs coconut trees, drills holes through the eye of a coconut with its powerful claws, and feeds on the coconut meat!

DOLPHIN

It's no wonder people often confuse marine dolphins and porpoises — after all, they look so much alike! True dolphins, however, have pointed snouts and cone-shaped teeth, while porpoises have more rounded snouts and flat-shaped teeth.

What You Need

❧ White paper
❧ Poster paint: light gray and light blue
❧ Fine black marker

What You Do

1 To print the dolphin's body, paint your palm and fingers light gray, leaving your thumb clean. Print horizontally in the center of the paper.

2 To form the dolphin's nose and tail, dip your pointer fingertip in light gray paint and print.

3 Form the dolphin's upper and lower fins using the length of your pointer finger dipped in gray paint.

4 To print ocean bubbles around the dolphin, dip your pointer fingertip in the light blue paint and dab spots here and there.

5 Outline and add details with a marker when dry.

Funny as it sounds, dolphins take naps while they swim. During the day and at night, dolphins nap for several minutes every couple of hours and open their eyes every now and then while sleeping.

Keeping Dolphins Safe

Dolphins are amazing divers — able to swim to depths of over 900 feet (277 m) and able to hold their breath for 6 minutes or longer! And marine biologists have determined that dolphins are among the most intelligent of all animal species, just behind monkeys and killer whales. Their habit of swimming with schools of tuna has gotten them into deadly trouble in years past, as they often become entangled in the purse nets fishermen use to catch tuna. Fortunately, many companies have decided not to sell or can tuna that's been caught by methods harmful to dolphins.

Be a Grocery Store Detective

Next time you're in the supermarket, do a little sleuthing on canned tuna. Most companies label their tuna "dolphin-safe" to show consumers that they use only tuna that was caught without harming dolphins. Take a look at the many varieties on the shelves. How many brands do you find that are dolphin-safe? How many brands don't have that symbol on their cans? You can make a difference by writing to the companies whose cans aren't labelled "dolphin-safe" and asking them to use only dolphin-safe tuna.

DOLPHIN-SAFE

SEAHORSE

Seahorses live in warm, shallow, tropical waters, and eat tiny crustaceans by rapidly sucking in water through their tubelike snouts.

What You Need

◗ White paper
◗ Poster paint: green and white
◗ Fine black marker

What You Do

1 Form the seahorse's head by painting your palm brown and printing close to the top of the paper.

2 To form the seahorse's body, paint your hand brown, leaving your thumb clean. Overlap the head a little as you print.

3 Print a nose using the length of your pointer finger.

4 To form the tail, dip a pointer fingertip into brown paint and make a curled row of prints.

5 Make a white eye with your pointer fingertip print.

6 Print some green seaweed using pointer fingertip prints.

7 Outline when dry; then add the eye's center, a mouth, and fins with a marker.

Funny Fact

The "horselike" head of a knight in a chess set resembles the seahorse's jointed armor.

"Marsupials" of the Sea

The seahorse is a weak swimmer. It moves about mainly by the rapid movement of its dorsal (back) fin, which acts as a propeller. The male seahorse has a kangaroo-like pouch into which the female places her eggs. The eggs are fertilized as they enter his pouch and remain there for 10 days until they hatch. At that time, the male bends his body this way and that, squirting out each baby, one-by-one.

Raise Some Brine Shrimp

Seahorses love to dine on tiny crustaceans like brine shrimp. Brine shrimp are very small and are perfect creatures to watch grow and can be easily grown from eggs in a jar. Purchase brine shrimp eggs from a tropical fish store; then sprinkle a pinch of eggs in a clean jar (do not use soap or detergent) filled with fresh sea water or salt water (6 level tablespoons [75 ml] of salt to 1 gallon [3.75 l] tap water). Place the jar in a warm spot, but not next to a direct source of heat like a radiator. The shrimp will hatch in a day or two and can be placed in a cool place. Use a magnifying glass to watch them swim. Shine a flashlight into the jar and what happens? Feed your shrimp a few drops of a dried yeast and warm water mixture each day.

LOBSTER

The American lobster can grow as long as 42 inches (107 cm) and weigh up to 45 pounds (20 kilograms). To reach that size a lobster needs to live about 100 years!

What You Need

- White paper
- Poster paint: brown, blue, green, and white
- Fine black marker

What You Do

1 To form the lobster's body, paint your palm brown and print.

2 To form the tail, paint the top 2 sections of your pointer finger brown and make several prints side-by-side, extending from the body.

3 Make the fantail, little flippers, and front leg sections using pointer fingertip prints.

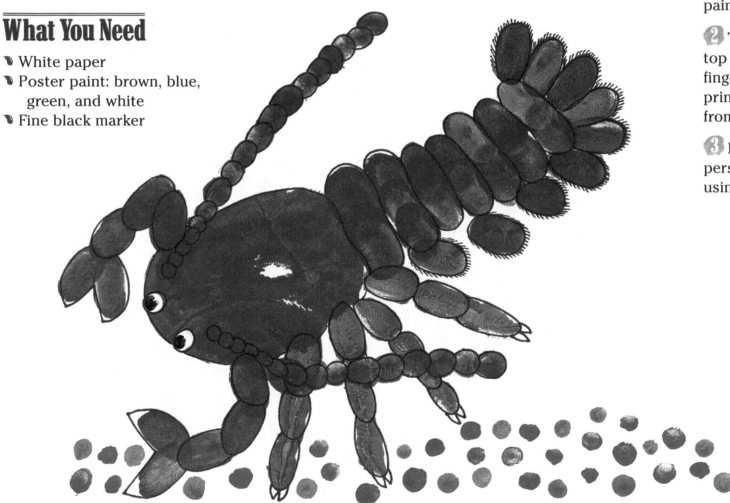

4 To print each claw on the 2 front legs, use 2 pointer fingertip prints. To print the 8 brown legs, use the length of your pointer finger.

5 To make the antennae, use your pinky dipped in brown paint and print a line of small dots. Make a pair of white eyes using fingerprints.

6 Add a design at the bottom of the paper using green and blue paint.

7 When dry, outline and add pupils, flippers, little hairs to the fantail, and little claws on the legs.

Look At My Claws

Lobsters are crustaceans, a group of creatures with segmented bodies, jointed legs, and hard shells. Lobsters have two pairs of antennae they use to search for food and to watch for enemies. They have five pairs of legs, two of which form large claws. The narrower of these claws, called the cutter, is used for slicing the lobster's favorite food, dead fish. The heavier claw, called the crusher, has toothlike bumps for crushing hard objects like shells.

Close-Up Crustaceans

While watching lobsters on the ocean floor is a rare experience, (some city aquariums do have lobsters), woodlice (also crustaceans) are easier to find and observe. Though many mistakenly believe they are insects, woodlice are more closely related to lobsters with their armored bodies and seven pairs of walking legs. Look beneath rocks and rotting wood in your backyard, at the edge of a park, or in a wooded area for these creatures. Or, lay a piece of wood on a damp, grassy, or muddy area and check in a few days for visitors. Touch one gently with a twig and what happens?

SEA ANEMONE

(see uh-nehm-uh-ne)

Crabs and other sea creatures use sea anemones as protection, swimming amid their tentacles when danger is near. Apparently these animals are immune to the anemone's nasty sting.

What You Need

- White paper
- Poster paint: black, pink, purple, orange, red, and yellow
- Fine black marker

What You Do

1 To form the base of your sea anemone, paint the length of your pointer finger orange and print 2 triangles end-to-end. Position your finger lengthwise and print 5 fingerprints fanning from one point to form each triangle.

2 To print the tentacles, paint the length of your pointer finger using all the colors except black.

3 Form some coral for your sea anemone to sit on using your pointer fingertip dipped in black, pink, and purple paint.

4 When dry, outline with a marker.

Silent Stingers

Although the sea anemone looks like a flower, it is actually an animal, not a plant. Sea anemones are usually still, but they can move around slowly. They often hide from prey by pulling in their tentacles and shortening their bodies to look like lumps on a rock. The anemone's mouth is surrounded by poisonous tentacles that paralyze prey with a sting before dragging it into its mouth for a tasty dinner.

Grow a Garden of "Anemones"

Did you know that some flowers are called anemones? They are related to the buttercups you may see growing in fields and along roadsides. Anemone flowers are often colorful like sea anemones, and can be grown in cool climates and partial shade. Just as the sea anemone's color attracts other creatures, colorful plants like zinnias, cosmos, and purple coneflowers, attract wildlife such as birds, butterflies, and insects. Visit a local nursery or garden center for ideas on your own garden of glorious anemones.

SHARK

Sharks are found all over the world, except in Antarctica, but they gather mostly in warm, tropical waters.

What You Need

- White paper
- Poster paint: brown, light and dark gray, white
- Fine black marker

What You Do

1 To print the shark's body, paint your palm, pointer finger, and middle finger light gray and your ring finger dark gray. Print horizontally in the center of your paper.

2 Form the shark's lower fin using the length of your pointer finger dipped in dark gray paint.

3 Print the shark's upper fin and tail using your pointer fingertip dipped in dark gray paint.

4 Make a rocky ocean floor using brown fingerprints. Print an eye using a white fingerprint.

5 When dry, outline and draw the gills, mouth, teeth, and an eye with a marker.

COOL COLOR OPTION

Have you ever heard of the tiger shark? Create one yourself by giving your shark print — you guessed it — tiger stripes!

Agile Swimmers

Sharks' bodies are made of flexible cartilage, not bone, which makes them especially agile. The whale shark, the largest fish in the ocean at 49 feet (15 m), has tiny teeth and an appetite for plankton and small fish. By eating weak, ailing, and wounded fish, they help the balance of life in the sea.

Make a "Shark's Tooth Necklace"

Sharks have reserve rows of teeth to continuously replace those they lose. Using clay, model some "shark's teeth" for a necklace. Give your teeth jagged-looking edges and pointed ends. Before setting out to dry, poke a hole with a toothpick through the top of each tooth. When dry, paint the teeth a grayish white. String onto a thin leather ribbon or yarn. Make up a fun story about the one that got away!

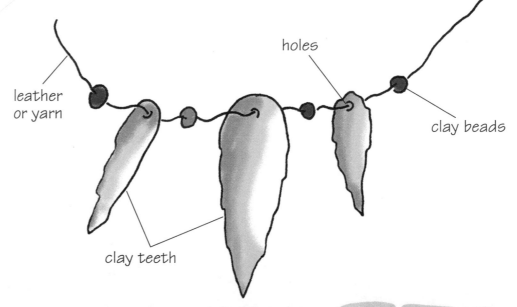

holes

leather or yarn

clay beads

clay teeth

WHALE

What do people mean when they say they had a "whale of a good time"? Judging by the size of these mammals, they would have had an enormous amount of fun!

What You Need

- White paper
- Poster paint: dark gray, white, green, and brown
- Fine black marker

What You Do

1 To print the whale's body, paint your palm and fingers dark gray, leaving your thumb clean; then print onto paper horizontally.

2 To form the tail and fin, use your pointer fingertip dipped in dark gray paint and print.

3 Print the seaweed and a few rocks using your pointer finger painted with green and brown paint.

4 Print an eye using a small white fingerprint.

5 Outline your whale and draw a mouth, teeth, and eye center with a marker.

Gentle Giants

The blue whale is the largest animal that has ever lived. It can measure up to 100 feet (30 m) in length and weigh nearly 288,000 pounds (130 metric tons)! Whales live in all oceans and seas of the world, but they do not have gills like fish. That's because whales are mammals and breathe air just like you. Some whales are good at holding their breath and can stay underwater for more than 50 minutes! The blowhole at the top of a whale's head is actually a nostril. Like all mammals, whales bear living young and nurse their babies. Scientists believe that whales communicate with each other by squealing and whistling and seem to enjoy breaching, or leaping out of the water.

Make a Comparison Chart

Making a chart that shows the similarities and differences between two animals can be helpful in keeping the two straight. Here's a chart to get you started on keeping track of the traitswhales and fish have in common and those they don't share.

Can you think of other examples? Are there other animal pairs you confuse? Make a comparison chart for them, too.

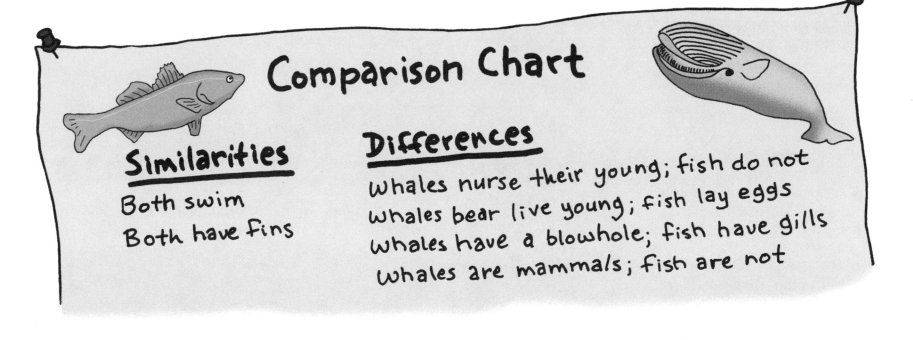

Comparison Chart

Similarities
Both swim
Both have fins

Differences
Whales nurse their young; fish do not
Whales bear live young; fish lay eggs
Whales have a blowhole; fish have gills
Whales are mammals; fish are not

FISH

Many states in the U.S. have fish hatcheries that raise trout, salmon, and other fish. In the spring, the adult fish are released into rivers to replenish their numbers in the wild.

What You Need

● White paper
● Poster paint: yellow and blue
● Fine black marker

What You Do

1 To print the fish's body, paint your entire hand with blue and yellow stripes. Print onto your paper, keeping your 3 middle fingers together and your thumb and pinky spread apart to form the fins.

2 To make the sandy ocean floor, use yellow fingerprints.

3 Make seaweed using the length of your pointer finger dipped in green paint. Print 3 times in the shape of a "V".

4 Dip your pointer finger in black paint to make the eye.

5 When the fish is dry, make a mouth, circle the eye, and outline the body using a marker.

Life In The Balance

Fish have been caught for food for as long as humans have walked the earth. They are cold-blooded animals, which means their body temperatures change to the temperature of the water they live in. Sadly, the number of endangered fish species has grown at an alarming rate because of careless humans who have polluted the oceans. For many years, the sea has been used as a dumping ground for waste materials, including garbage from ships and shoreline factories. Next time you visit the beach, lake, or stream, help out the fish — and other creatures that rely on water — by picking up any litter you see there.

Look at My Scales

Visit your local fish market or super-market and ask the meat clerk for a few fish scales, or scrape some off a fish you've caught or found on the

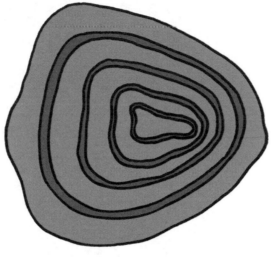

beach (always wash your hands after handling fish). With a magnifying glass, look closely for the wide, light-colored bands that show the growth of the fish over the summer. Now look for the dark, narrow bands that show the fish's growth during the winter. Each dark and light band equals one year of the fish's life. Count the dark and light bands to figure out the age of the fish.

Funny Fact

The endangered spotted hand fish rarely swims, but instead walks along the sea floor on its fins. It resembles the human hand and can be found in the waters off southeast Tasmania.

SQUID

Squid are mollusks, soft-bodied animals with hard shells or shell-like coverings. They're usually found in shallow shoals off the eastern coast of the United States.

What You Need

- White paper
- Poster paint: peach and white
- Fine black marker

What You Do

1 To print the squid's body, paint your palm with peach-colored paint and print close to the bottom left of the paper.

2 Print the squid's head using your 3 middle fingers painted peach.

3 To make the squid's 8 arms, print the length of your middle finger painted peach.

4 Form the tentacles by printing rows of pointer fingertip prints. Print a white eye using your fingertip.

5 When dry, outline and add details to the eye and small suction cups on the end of the tentacles and the underside of the arms with a marker.

Funny Fact

When threatened, a squid can change its color and markings rapidly to blend in with its surroundings. How's that for a disguise!

OOEY, GOOEY, CREEPY, CRAWLY BUGS

LADYBUG

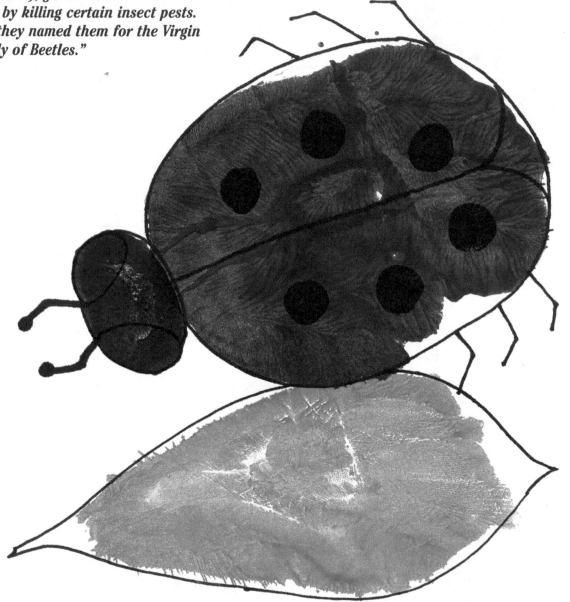

During the Middle Ages (from 476 to 1450 A.D.), gardeners noticed these colorful little beetles defended their crops by killing certain insect pests. They liked these helpful beetles so much, they named them for the Virgin Mary, who was sometimes called "Our Lady of Beetles."

What You Need

❥ White paper
❥ Poster paint: red, green, and black
❥ Fine black marker

What You Do

1 To make the body, paint your palm red and print in the center of the paper.

2 To make the leaf, paint your palm green and print just below the red handprint.

3 Print the head using your thumb dipped in black paint.

4 Give your ladybug some spots using your pointer finger dipped in black paint.

5 When dry, give your ladybug 2 antennae and 6 legs. Outline the shape if you wish.

Ladybug, Ladybug, Fly Away Home!

Ladybugs aren't really true bugs — they're beetles. Their brightly colored shells serve to warn potential predators of their awful taste. In cold climates, adult ladybugs hibernate in safe, warm places and live through the winter. Ladybugs are a gardener's best friend because they eat aphids, scale insects, and other plant pests. In fact, they will eat 15 aphids a day — no slouch when you consider the damage those aphids can do to a row of plants.

Get Rid of Garden Pests Naturally

Invite a ladybug to live in your own organic garden — rent free! An organic garden is grown without the use of poisonous pesticides or fertilizers. Instead of using insecticides on your tomatoes, which kill helpful as well as harmful insects, use a natural pest avenger like garlic juice spray. Its pungent odor will be enough to chase away even the hungriest aphids. Planting marigolds around your garden is another super way to prevent pests from visiting. Even hungry rabbits can't stand the smell of these flowering beauties!

In pioneer days, having ladybugs hibernating in your house was thought to be a sign of good luck.

GRASSHOPPER

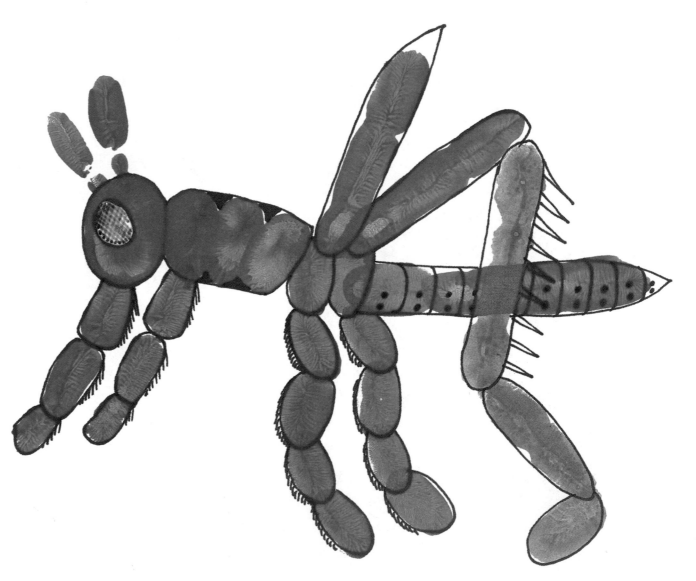

Grasshoppers can jump 3 feet (.91 m) high. That's nearly 40 times their height!

What You Need

❧ White paper
❧ Poster paint: green, pink, and white
❧ Fine black marker

What You Do

1 To print the grasshopper's head, use your thumb dipped in green paint and print toward the left of the paper.

2 Print 5 green body sections, leading from the head toward the right, using your pointer finger. Paint your longest finger green and print the rest of the grasshopper's body.

3 Print the wing and first section of its hind leg using the length of your longest finger.

4 Print the 2 front legs using the length of your pointer finger painted green. Form the 2 center legs (with 4 prints for each leg), using green pointer fingertip prints.

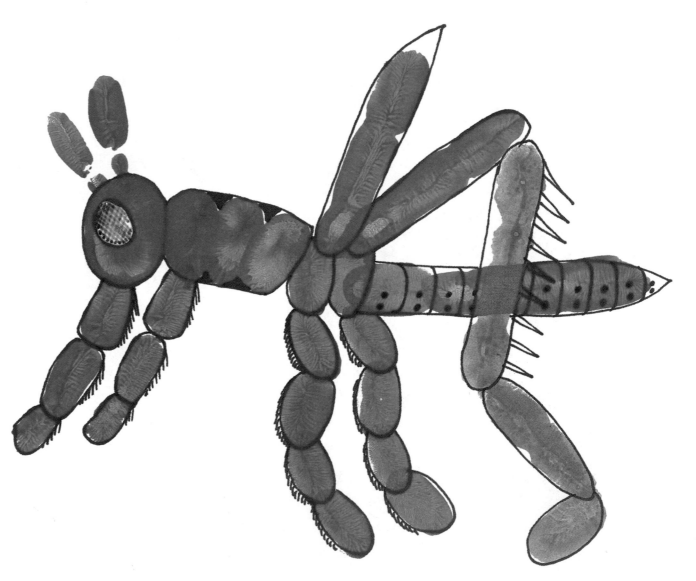

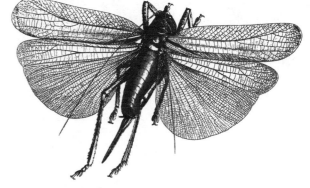

5 For the antennae, dip the side of your pinky in green paint and print on top of its head.

6 Print a white eye using your pointer fingertip. Print the second section of the grasshopper's hind leg, using your pointer finger painted pink.

7 Print the third section of the hind leg, using only the top 2 sections of your pointer finger painted pink. Then, make the foot using a pointer fingertip print.

8 When dry, outline with a marker. Add details to the eye, hairs to the legs, spikes to the hind legs, and stripes and dots to the grasshopper's tail.

Hop, Skip, and Jump

Locusts are a type of short-horned grasshopper that have been known to cause lots of damage to crops when they swarm, or gather. If geographical conditions are bad for a certain type of grasshopper, they'll flee in enormous numbers, often travelling hundreds of miles in a few days. Their swarms can be so large, they are sometimes sighted by radar.

Use Chirping Crickets As a Thermometer

Crickets are closely related to grasshoppers. You may know them best by the chirping they do on hot, summer nights. Believe it or not, you can tell roughly what the temperature is outside by listening to their chirps. Just count the number of chirps a cricket makes in one minute; then divide that number by four and add forty. Your result should be within two to three degrees of the air temperature. Check a real thermometer to see how close the cricket came to "telling" the temperature.

Funny Fact

Band-winged grasshoppers sing by snapping their hind legs while flying.

BUMBLEBEE

Listen to a bee hum as it "bumbles" into flowers—it was this humming that gave it its name. In Middle English, which was spoken hundreds of years ago, the word bumblen means "to hum"!

What You Need

❧ White paper
❧ Poster paint: blue, black, and yellow
❧ Fine black marker

What You Do

1 To make the bee's body, paint your palm and fingers with black and yellow stripes and print onto paper.

2 Print the bee's wings using your thumb dipped into blue paint.

3 Print 2 eyes with your pointer fingertip dipped in black paint.

4 When dry, outline with a marker.

Nectar Gatherers

You may be very familiar with bumblebees and honey bees, which feed on flower nectar and honey. Nectar, which is made into honey by bees, is the sugary substance produced at the base of a flower's petals. Bees have branched, feathery body hairs and females have "brushes" on their legs, which they use to brush off the pollen from the hairs. Bees store pollen on their bellies and hind legs and take it back to the nest, but along the way they can pollinate hundreds of flowers — in turn, helping our plants to grow.

Five Ways to Avoid Being Stung

Here are a few things you can do to avoid being stung by bees and wasps,

whose venomous stings can be deadly to those allergic to them.

- Avoid bright-colored clothing, because bees are attracted to bright colors.
- Stand still when a bee, wasp, or yellowjacket comes near you. Swatting at bees will only make them mad.
- Leave wasps, hornets, and bees alone on a cloudy day or in early fall when they are very busy.
- Always stay away from small holes in the ground, where bees may nest, especially during springtime.
- Never disturb a nest or hive unless it has been abandoned for winter.

Naturally Speaking

A BEE'S TONGUE IS LONGER THAN A WASP'S AND IS BETTER SUITED FOR GATHERING NECTAR FROM A GREATER VARIETY OF FLOWERS.

BEETLE

Beetles live all over the earth, except in the oceans. They live in rainforests, deserts, freezing-cold areas, and hot springs. Even mountain lakes and polluter sewers are popular homes for beetles!

What You Need

❥ White paper
❥ Poster paint: gray and white
❥ Fine black marker

What You Do

1 To print the beetle's head, paint your palm gray and print in the center of the paper. Form the base of the head using a gray thumbprint.

2 Print the forward part of the beetle's head using a pointer fingertip.

3 Print the antennae using your pinky fingertip.

4 Make the leg sections using pointer fingertip prints.

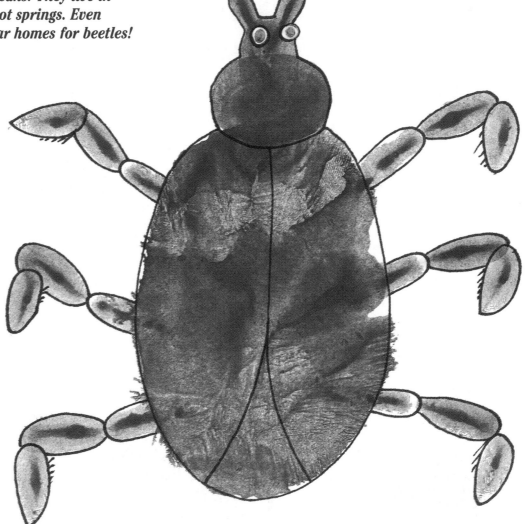

5 Print some white eyes using your pinky fingertip.

6 When dry, outline with a marker, adding little hairs to the feet and a line to divide the wings.

Meet The Beetles

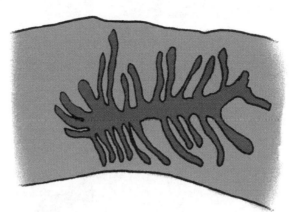

Beetles were considered symbols of everlasting life by the people of ancient Egypt. One kind of beetle, the scarab, was even used to create beautiful jewelry such as pendants and necklaces. Beetles eat flowers, seeds, fruits, and wood for food, but some species feed on other small animals and insects. The bark beetle is known for destroying elm trees and conifers by spreading a disease called Dutch Elm.

Look For Beetle Tracks in Bark

In your backyard, the woods, or a park, look for a piece of bark on the ground or on a fallen limb. If you have a fallen limb, gently peel off the bark. Look for tunnels, or nurseries, under the bark where adult beetles previously laid their eggs. You can see how when the beetle larvae feed and grow, they create lines in the bark. Look for the tiny holes in the bark where the beetles emerged when they became adults.

COOL COLOR OPTION

Some types of beetles are luminescent, so get out your glow-in-the-dark and fluorescent-colored paints and go bug wild!

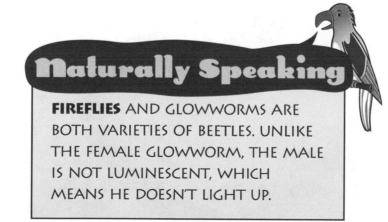

Naturally Speaking

FIREFLIES AND GLOWWORMS ARE BOTH VARIETIES OF BEETLES. UNLIKE THE FEMALE GLOWWORM, THE MALE IS NOT LUMINESCENT, WHICH MEANS HE DOESN'T LIGHT UP.

CENTIPEDE

Centipedes have long, flat, wormlike bodies and 15 or more pairs of legs. Some of the 2,800 species of centipedes have up to 177 pairs of legs!

What You Need

- White paper
- Poster paint: brown, green, and tan
- Fine black marker

What You Do

1 Print the long shape of a centipede using your pointer fingertip dipped in brown paint.

2 Print a few rocks around the cetipede with your pointer fingertip dipped in tan paint.

3 Print some grass growing between the rocks using the length of your pinky.

4 When dry, outline each section of your centipede. Where each section meets the next, draw in a pair of thin legs.

5 Form a pair of antennae by drawing lots of little circles. Print a pair of fingerprint eyes.

Tip: For younger children, draw a light pencil line to follow.

Tiny, But Powerful Jaws

Centipedes live all over the world, hiding during the day and hunting for small invertebrates, such as insects and worms, at night. All centipedes have poisonous jaws for paralyzing their prey. Small centipedes are harmless to humans, but some large species have a painful bite that allows them to paralyze prey as big as mice, lizards, and large insects.

Take a Centipede Walk

Invite a friend to play this game. Have your friend blindfold you and then guide you slowly on a short walk. Listen to, smell, and feel your surroundings along the way. Touch the

grass and the trees. Do you smell anything special here and there? Now, stop and take off the blindfold. See if you can trace your way back to where you started your walk by listening, feeling, and smelling your surroundings like a centipede. Were you able to find your way back home?

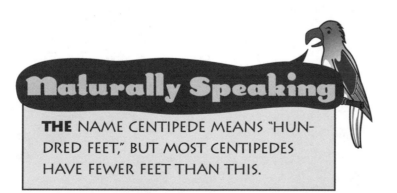

Naturally Speaking

THE NAME CENTIPEDE MEANS "HUNDRED FEET," BUT MOST CENTIPEDES HAVE FEWER FEET THAN THIS.

ANTS

Ants are related to wasps and bees and live in colonies of up to 20 million. That's more than all the people who live in Australia!

What You Need

- White paper
- Poster paint: red and black
- Ruler
- Fine black marker

What You Do

1 Make a grid of vertical and horizontal lines on your paper for the tablecloth. Print in every other square, using your thumb dipped in red paint. Let dry.

2 Form the black abdomens (tail end) of the ants with thumbtip prints.

3 Form the black thorax (center part) of each ant with a pointer fingertip print.

4 Print the ants' heads in black, using your pinky fingertip.

5 Give each ant 6 legs and a pair of antennae, using a marker.

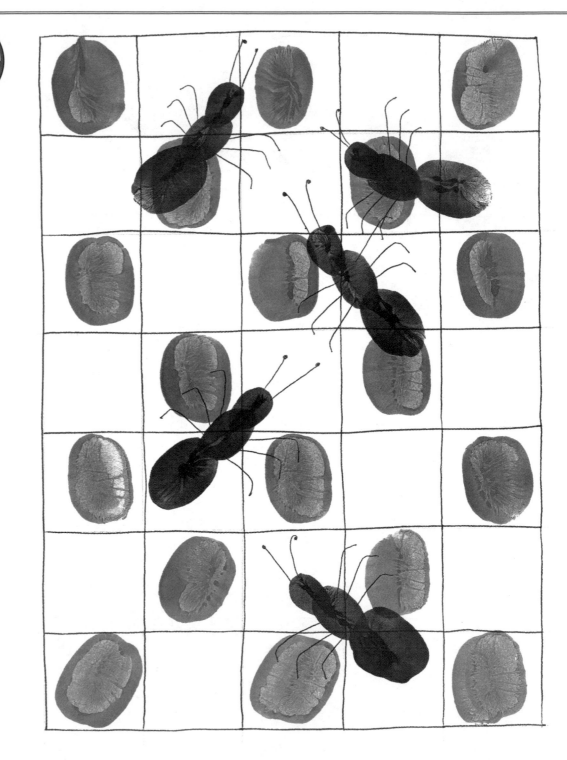

FOREST & BACKYARD WILDLIFE

FROG

Some kinds of frogs spend all of their time in the water, never coming out to dry land. Others spend most of their time on land requiring only the moisture from under leaves and rocks.

What You Need

- White paper
- Poster paint: light and dark green, pink
- Fine black marker

What You Do

1 To print the frog's body and 4 legs, paint your whole hand (except thumb) green and print, fingers facing downward, at the top part of the paper.

2 Print the lilypads, using your palm only, painted light green.

3 Print the 5 petals of the lilypad flower, using your pointer finger dipped in pink paint.

4 Fingerprint 2 white eyes.

5 When dry, complete the eyes, draw a mouth, and outline the flowers.

Ribbit Ribbit, Croak Croak

Even though they may look and act alike, there are many differences between frogs and toads. Both are amphibians, which means they spend part of their lives in water breathing through gills like fish and part of their lives above water breathing air through lungs like you. If you look closely at a frog's skin, you'll see that it's shiny, smooth, and moist, while a toad's is bumpy, rough, and dry.

Take a Leap

A common bullfrog can leap as far as 6 feet (1.83 meters). Professional long jumpers like Mike Powell, who jumped 29 feet and 4 $1/2$ inches at the 1991 World Championship in Tokyo, Japan, spend their days training to leap great distances. See how far you can jump on a grassy area. Mark a line by out-stretching a length of jump rope on the grass; then back up 10 paces and run to the marked line, jumping as far as you can from it. Use a tape measure to determine the length of your leap. Measure from your heels back to the jump line. Can you leap as far as a bullfrog?

ANIMAL ANTICS

The Australian frog broods its eggs in the stomach and coughs up froglets at birth. Ick!

BAT

Bats are found all over North America and love to dine on insects — especially mosquitoes. One bat can eat as many as 600 mosquitoes in an hour! How's that for nature's bug repellent?

What You Need

- White paper
- Poster paint: black, brown, and white
- Fine black marker

What You Do

1 To form the bat's wings, paint both hands black, leaving your thumbs clean. Print, overlapping slightly in the center to form the body.

2 Make 2 feet and 2 ears, using brown fingerprints.

3 Fingerprint 2 white eyes.

4 When dry, outline the bat's ears and feet and give it some claws and small black pupils in its eyes.

Mysterious and Misunderstood

Many people believe all sorts of silly bat tales, most of which are untrue. Bats don't fly in your hair, as many people think. They're just darting at mosquitoes looking to feast on YOU! More than 40 species of bats in North America make their homes in caves, hollow trees, foliage, rock crevices, and small spaces around buildings. In some caves in the American Southwest there live millions of Mexican free-tailed bats!

Set Up a Bat House

Setting up a bat house is a great way to keep bats in your neck of the woods. There are several conservation organizations that sell bat houses (write Bat Conservation International, P.O. Box 162603, Austin, TX 78716 for more information on purchasing plans for building bat houses or to buy a bat house). Bats are known to be shy and fussy homeowners, so it may be difficult at first to attract bats to your property. Don't get discouraged, though; sometimes putting up more than one bat house can be helpful. Once your bat house has been up for awhile, stand close by and listen for bats squeaking. Always remember the importance of respecting a bat's home — and other wildlife homes — as bats are easily frightened.

SNAKE

Snakes, the world's limbless reptiles, are perhaps one of the most feared wild creatures. That's too bad, because many species are harmless. Snakes are also very important predators of rodents and insects and play a vital role in our environment.

What You Need

❥ White paper
❥ Poster paint: black, brown, white, and yellow
❥ Fine black marker

What You Do

1 Form the snake shape by dipping your pointer finger first in black, then brown, then yellow paint and printing connected fingerprints in a curly design. Make the yellow prints narrow, using the side of your finger.

2 Fingerprint 2 white eyes.

3 When dry, outline with marker.

A Snake's Way of Knowing

A snake's flickering tongue is not harmful to people or animals. It's just the snake's way of detecting the body scent of other animals. Because snakes don't have ears, they cannot hear airborne sounds, but they are able to detect sound through vibrations in the ground.

Sculpt a Salt Dough Snake

Roll a lump of salt dough back and forth between your palms until it forms a snake shape the length and thickness you want (see dough recipe on page 71). Wet your hands if the snake starts to crack. Let your snake dry on waxed paper in a warm, dry place for 2 or 3 days. Check out a book from the library on snakes and look for pictures of colorful snakes. Use these designs as inspiration for painting your snakes with tempera or acrylic paints. When dry, paint your snake with clear nail polish for a glossy shine.

Naturally Speaking

MORE PEOPLE ARE HARMED EACH YEAR BY BEE, WASP, AND SCORPION STINGS THAN BY SNAKE BITES. FEWER THAN 300 OF THE 2,550 TO 3,000 SPECIES OF SNAKE ARE HARMFUL TO HUMANS.

OWL

Owls have extraordinary hearing, but their ears aren't visible to us. Though some owls appear to have large ears, the soft feathers that stick out from their heads are actually called ear tufts.

What You Need

- White paper
- Poster paint: yellow, gray, blue, black, brown
- Fine black marker

What You Do

1 To paint the owl's body, paint your hand gray and print at the top of your page, fingers facing downward. Spread out your thumb and pinky to form the wings, and keep your 3 middle fingers together.

2 Print a brown branch just below the owl, using your tallest finger. Use fingerprints for the small branches.

3 Print 2 yellow eyes using your fingerprints.

4 Form the beak by dipping the side of the tip of your pinky in black and using a black fingerprint for the center of the eyes.

5 Outline with marker when dry.

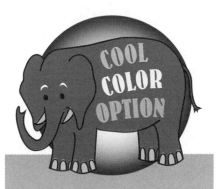

COOL COLOR OPTION

Owls are incredibly beautiful with their white and gray feathers, but you can create a colorful owl using a variety of soft colors like pale yellow, rose, or light silver. Be inventive.

Bring On The Night

Most owls are nocturnal, which means they are active at night. Because of their soft feathers, owls can fly very quietly to surprise their prey. Owls rely mostly on their incredible hearing when hunting. Their ears are asymmetrical (different from one another), so the owl hears sounds from above with one ear, while the other distinguishes sounds from below. Because of this, an owl can hear just where its prey is on the ground below.

A Game of Owl and Mouse

An owl can hear a mouse squeak from a half mile (0.8 km) away! How does your hearing compare to an owl's? Play this game with a friend and hear for yourself. Find a toy that squeaks when you squeeze it or use two spoons. Go outside and stand with your back to your partner. Then, have your friend walk away from you while squeaking the toy or clacking the two spoons together. Raise your hand when you can no longer hear the noise. Turn around to see the distance between you and your partner, which is how far you could hear. Now, ask a grown-up to show you how far a half mile is from where you live. If you were an owl, that's how far away you could hear a mouse!

PORCUPINE

The Latin name for porcupine means "the pig with thorns." Porcupines don't have thorns, of course, they have quills — more than 30,000 of them!

What You Need

- White paper
- Poster paint: brown, black
- Fine black marker

What You Do

1 To form the body and a few spines, paint your hand brown, leaving your thumb clean; then print onto paper.

2 Add more quills using your fingers dipped in brown paint. Add 4 legs using your fingertips.

3 Fingerprint a black nose and an eye.

4 When dry, outline the face, legs, and body with marker and add some whiskers.

A Prickly Proposition

Porcupines are well known for their long, sharp quills. Not many animals dare attack porkies, because of their "sharp" defenses, but no doubt you've heard of a curious dog getting stuck with a face full of quills! Porcupines don't actually throw their quills, of course, they use them only in self-defense when threatened by another animal. Porcupine quills are barbed like fish hooks, so when they touch a threatening predator, they lodge in the victim's skin and come loose from the porcupine.

Porcupine Sculptures

Create a salt dough porcupine by mixing together 1 $\frac{1}{2}$ cups (375 ml) salt, 4 cups (1 l) flour, and 1 $\frac{1}{2}$ cups (375 ml) water.

Knead the mixture well, adding extra water if too crumbly. Next, shape the dough into a porcupine figure. Use whole toothpicks to cover it with long quills and half toothpicks for shorter quills. Leave the head bare. Add furry details to the head by running a comb over the clay. Use beans for the eyes and nose. Mold little feet from the clay. Allow to harden in a warm, dry place.

Give your porcupine multicolored quills and make it the fanciest porcupine ever to roam the woods!

BEAR

There are several types of bears in North America, including black, brown, and polar bears. Brown bears, such as the grizzly and coastal brownie, can only be found in Alaska, Canada, and in a few National Parks in the American west.

What You Need

- White paper
- Poster paint: black, orange/gold, and white
- Fine black marker

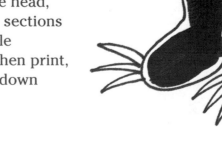

What You Do

1 To print the bear's body, paint your hand black, leaving your thumb clean; then print horizontally onto paper with your fingers pointing left. Leave enough room at the left for the bear's head.

2 To make the head, paint the top 2 sections of your 3 middle fingers black; then print, pointing them down slightly.

3 To make the front legs, paint the top 2 sections of your pointer finger black and print.

4 Print the ears and front paws using your pointer fingertip dipped in black paint. To form the bear's back legs, use 2 fingerprints.

5 Print the golden snout using pointer fingertip prints. Form the bear's crest with orange/gold thumb and pointer fingerprints.

6 To make the nose, dip your pointer fingertip into black paint and print.

7 Form an eye with a white fingertip print. Make the nose and the eye with black fingerprints.

8 Outline and add claws and whiskers.

Light Sleepers

Bears do hibernate, but they aren't the deep sleepers that people mistakenly believe them to be. Like other hibernating animals, a bear's heartbeat slows down to save energy, but bears often wake up throughout the winter and sometimes even leave their dens briefly to roam on a warm day.

Hang it Up

Only black bears can climb trees, but that doesn't mean other types of bears aren't clever at getting something they want — especially if it smells and tastes good! If you plan to go camping in bear country, knowing how to "bear-proof" your campsite is important. To "bear bag" your food, toss a rope with a bag of food tied to one end over a tree limb, several feet away from the trunk, and several yards from where you will be sleeping. Pull the loose end to haul the bag up to the branch and then tie a second food bag as high on the other end of the rope as possible. Leave a loop at the bottom. Using a long stick, balance the bags side-by-side and retrieve them by hooking the loop with the stick and pulling it down. Remember, never leave food or anything with a scent in your backpack or take food into your tent.

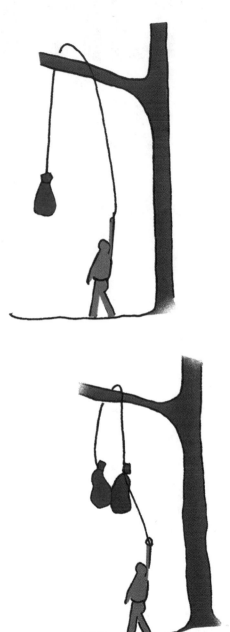

TURTLE

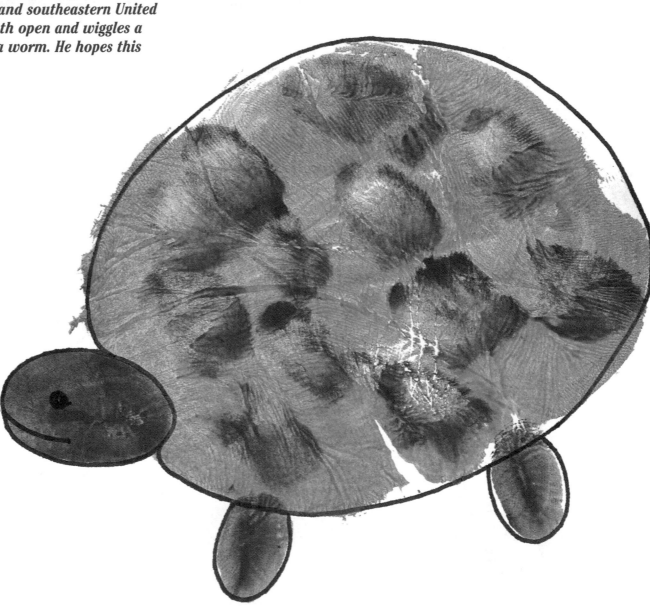

The alligator snapping turtle of central and southeastern United States sits under the water with its mouth open and wiggles a projection on its tongue that looks like a worm. He hopes this will lure an innocent fish — for lunch!

What You Need

❥ White paper
❥ Poster paint: brown and green
❥ Fine black marker

What You Do

1 To make the turtle's body, paint your palm green, adding a few brown spots here and there. Print onto the center of your paper.

2 Make the head using your thumbtip dipped in brown paint.

3 Form the feet using your pointer finger dipped into brown paint.

4 When dry, outline with marker.

Endangered Means Forever

About 30 species of turtles are endangered, which means they are in danger of becoming extinct or gone forever. Some turtles have been collected for their meat and millions of marine turtle eggs are collected each year for food or oil. The shell of the hawksbill turtle is still in demand, even though it's endangered. Many turtles become endangered because their nests are destroyed by careless humans when clearing land for construction. If you are concerned about endangered turtles, contact the National Wildlife Federation for information on how you can help.

Count My Plates

If you have a pet turtle or know someone who does, take a look at its shell (never approach turtles in the wild without a grown-up who knows about turtles). Use a magnifying glass to get a close look at the shell and count the rims or rings on the turtle's shell plates. Each rim or ring equals one year. Some turtles live to be 20 or 30 years old, and giant turtles live even longer. How many rings do you see?

SNAIL

The snail is a shelled mollusk that's actually related to the octopus. A snail will hide in its spiral shell when afraid and has a flattened foot that moves it along.

What You Need

❧ White paper
❧ Poster paint: dark brown, orange/brown, light blue, and black
❧ Fine black marker

What You Do

1. Draw a spiral shape at the top of the paper. Follow the spiral, using your pointer fingertip dipped in dark brown paint.

2. Fill in the snail's shell using orange/brown pointer fingertip prints.

3. To make the snail's head and tail, paint the length of your pointer finger dark brown and print.

4. Print 2 thin tentacles on the snail's head, using the side of your pinky. At the top of each tentacle, print a small, black circle using your pointer fingertip.

5. Print a ground scene using your pointer finger. Print 2 eyes at the top center of each tentacle with your pointer fingertip.

6. Outline when dry, and draw a small pair of tentacles beside the larger ones.

A Snail's Pace

Snails carry their houses on their backs so it's no wonder they move very slowly — you would, too! They have a pair of large tentacles on their heads that help them feel their way around and also help them see. Snails also travel using their one foot that is equipped with a slime gland at the front that secretes mucus on whatever the snail moves on.

Construct a Snail Hideaway

Snails like to hide out in cool, dark, damp places so it's relatively easy to attract them. Just find a clay flowerpot and decorate it with acrylic paint designs. Place the pot on its side in a grassy or leafy area and check it daily to see if a snail has crawled in. Put your snail on a piece of plastic wrap and watch it from underneath. Do you see its foot rippling as it slides along? Put a dab of bright, nontoxic waterproof paint on the snail's shell before setting it free, then you can see if it returns.

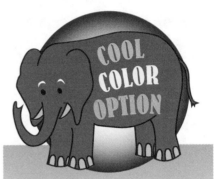

Handprint a colorful shell for your snail and add a silvery trail of glitter.

SKUNK

Skunks are nocturnal (see page 80) and eat plants and small animals during the night. They live in burrows and some species live in trees.

What You Need

- White paper
- Poster paint: black and white
- Fine black marker

What You Do

1 To form the body of your skunk, paint your hand black and print toward the right of the paper. Point your thumb upward to form part of the tail.

2 To print the skunk's face, paint a black leaf shape on your palm and print.

3 Make the ears, the legs, and a bushy tail using your pointer fingertip dipped in black paint. Let dry completely.

4 To make the stripes, print 2 rows of white fingerprints along the back, tail, and down the center of the skunk's face. Print a white fingerprint for each eye; then add a black fingerprint to the center of each eye.

5 When dry, draw the eyelashes and whiskers and outline if you wish.

There is a plant that grows in wet places in Eastern North America that has large, broad, veiny leaves and smells like a skunk. It's called—you guessed it— "skunk cabbage"!

PEE-EWE!

The skunk belongs to the weasel family and is found all over the western hemisphere. You probably know it best by its strong-smelling scent, which it often sprays in self-defense. If a skunk is disturbed, it ejects a pungent spray from two glands at the base of its tail. A skunk can send a blast of spray up to 12 feet (4 m) away. Quite often, a skunk will hiss or growl as a warning before spraying. Since skunks can carry the rabies virus, it's never safe to handle them.

Pet Weigh-In

A common striped skunk weighs between 1 1/2 and 5 1/2 pounds (.75 and 2.5 kg). But how do you suppose scientists who study skunks and other wildlife collect all their information about them? It takes hours of watching and waiting and close study. Quite often, it's necessary to safely trap animals to weigh and measure them. Luckily, you can figure out how to weigh "wildlife" in your home much more easily. Weigh your cat, rabbit, or small dog by stepping onto a scale while holding your pet. Record the weight. Then, put your pet down and record how much you weigh alone. Subtract the second reading from the first and you'll know how much your pet weighs.

RACCOON

Raccoons are nocturnal animals, which means they sleep during the day and are active at night. Their name harkens back to the Native American word for this masked creature, arakunem (ah-rah-KOO-nem).

What You Need

🐾 White paper
🐾 Poster paint: tan and black
🐾 White chalk
🐾 Fine black marker

What You Do

1 To print the raccoon's body, paint your palm tan and print toward the left of the paper.

2 To make the front of the raccoon, paint your palm tan again and print, overlapping the body slightly.

3 Form the raccoon's back leg, using a tan thumbprint. To form the 2 front legs, paint the top 2 sections of your pointer finger tan and print.

4 Form the tail by printing a row of tan fingerprints, leaving a space between each print. Fill each space with a black fingerprint.

5 Print the black eyes, ears, and nose, using your pointer fingertip.

6 When dry, shade around the ears, eyes, and nose with white chalk. Draw a small white circle on the black ring around the eyes. Outline, and add claws and whiskers.

ANIMAL ANTICS

Raccoons are known to wash their food before eating it, but it's not because they want to clean the food they're eating. Raccoons, by instinct, dunk their food in water in order to soften it for chewing and swallowing.

Masked Bandits

Raccoons are *omnivorous*, which means they eat both meat and plants. Actually, raccoons will eat just about anything they can find and especially love raiding garbage cans. You can identify them by the dark rings on their tails and their black-masked faces that serve as camouflage. You should never approach and handle raccoons because they are likely to carry the rabies virus during an epidemic. If you see a raccoon acting strangely, call your local animal shelter or state department of wildlife.

Make a Mask

Paint your palms black and print onto a paper plate, poster board, or an old greeting card so the heels of your hands are end-to-end, fingers facing outward. When dry, cut out 2 small eye holes. Cut around the palm prints. Cut a strip of elastic or paper to fit snugly around your head; then staple one end to the edge of each side of the mask.

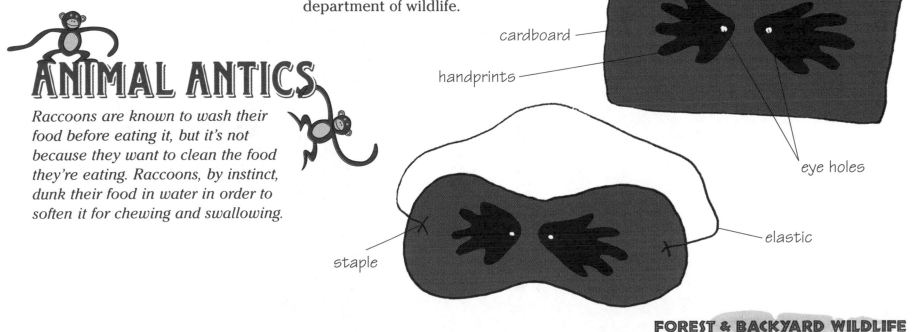

cardboard

handprints

eye holes

staple

elastic

MOOSE

The moose is the largest member of the deer family and lives in many regions of northern North America, including Alaska, Canada, several western states, and northern New England.

What You Need

🞂 White paper
🞂 Poster paint: brown, tan, green, and black
🞂 Fine black marker

What You Do

1 To print the head, paint palms and four fingers dark brown. Print facing fingers toward the bottom of the page.

2 Form the tan antlers using your four fingers. Print the lower antler point with your pointer fingertip.

3 Form the brown ears with thumbtip prints. Form the eyes and nostrils with black pointer fingerprints.

4 Print some long, green grass using the length of your pointer finger. Outline the moose with fine black marker.

A Wild Life

Moose are massive animals with long legs, a big head, enormous antlers, and an elongated, overhanging muzzle. They can weigh up to 1,800 pounds (825 kg), about as much as a small car! They live in moist woods of willows, poplars, and birch and wade into lakes to feed on water plants. Female moose give birth to one, often two, and sometimes three calves in late spring. When calves are a year old, they are driven away by their mothers so she may give birth to new calves.

Chocolate Moose Truffles

Mix 2 ounces (56 gm) each of the following ingredients into a bowl: cocoa powder, confectioners' sugar, chopped nuts, and cream cheese. Roll into about 40 balls. Roll balls in chocolate sprinkles or powder. Make a nose with a chocolate chip and eyes with raisins. Dip mini pretzel "antlers" in 6 ounces (168 gm) melted chocolate and let cool on waxed paper. Place right side up on each moose truffle.

Funny Fact

A moose's huge rack of antlers can weigh as much as 50 pounds (22.5 kg.)! That's like balancing a giant bag of dog food on your head for most of your life.

RED FOX

While sleeping in its den, a red fox wraps its tail, or brush, around itself, using it as a soft, fluffy scarf while curled up.

What You Need

- White paper
- Poster paint: orange, white, and black
- Fine black marker

What You Do

1. To form the head and snout, paint your palm, your pointer finger, and longest finger orange and print diagonally with fingers facing downward.

2. Print the fox's neck by painting your palm orange, then printing at an angle from the fox's head.

3. To form the ears, dip your thumb in white paint and print.

4 To add some white fur beneath the chin, use pointer fingertip prints.

5 To form a nose, dip your pointer finger in black paint and print.

6 To make the eyes, dip your pointer finger in orange paint and print twice.

7 When dry, add the details to the ears and neck with a marker. Add eyelashes and whiskers on the nose and above the eyes, and outline if you wish.

A Beautiful Tail

The red fox is a member of the dog family and is an agile predator. It looks bigger than it is because of its long tail and legs, and thick fur. In fact, the fox only weighs 10-15 pounds (4-7 kg) when fully grown. A mama fox's beautiful tail, or brush, is used as a signal for her pups to follow her. The tip is white and when held high pups can see it and won't get lost. A fox's tail also helps it keep its balance.

Let's Go Tracking

Springtime is a great time to go tracking. Ask a grown-up to take you into the woods or to a pond, lake, or stream to look for fox tracks in the mud. You may want to take along a nature guide that shows what the tracks of foxes and other wildlife look like. If you want to make a plaster cast of your prints, take along plaster of paris and water to mix in a coffee can (read package directions first). Look for paw prints in the dirt or mud.

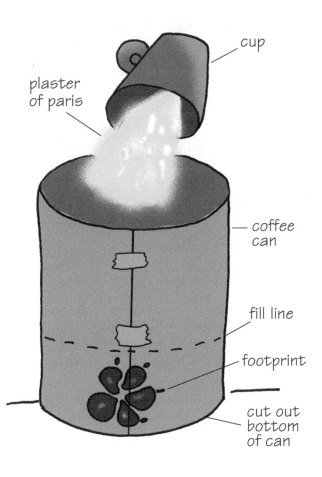

cup
plaster of paris
coffee can
fill line
footprint
cut out bottom of can

For casts, gently pour the plaster into the print and let harden. No fox prints? Try looking for other prints like those from a rabbit, squirrel, or your dog or cat.

SQUIRREL

Just about wherever you live in North America, squirrels can be seen scurrying to and from all kinds of places. Look for them in city parks or climbing up and down trees — and birdfeeders! — in country settings.

What You Need

- White paper
- Poster paint: light and dark brown, gray
- Fine black marker

What You Do

1 To form the head, paint a leaf shape on your palm with gray paint and print close to the top of your paper.

2 To print the squirrel's body, paint your hand gray, leaving the thumb clean. Overlap the head a little.

3 Print a branch beneath the squirrel, using the length of your pointer finger painted dark brown.

4 Give the squirrel a nose and ear and print the base of an acorn, using a dark brown fingertip print.

5 Fingerprint an eye and an acorn, using light brown paint.

6 Print the squirrel's gray foot using your pointer fingertip. To print an arm holding the acorn, use your whole pointer finger.

7 To form the tail, use gray paint on your pointer finger and print several times in a row. Repeat with light brown paint.

8 Outline when dry. Add the details to the tail, whiskers, claws, and eyes.

COOL COLOR OPTION

All squirrels are not gray. Some are a deep reddish-brown. Add a little color to squirrel prints by using a combination of reds, browns, and grays.

Squirrel Away

Gray squirrels live in the eastern half of the United States and in some parts of the Pacific states as well. They nest in tree hollows and leaf nests high in trees. During the summer and fall, they store food for winter by burying seeds and nuts such as black walnuts, butternuts, and hickories.

Go On a Nut Hunt— Squirrel-Style

Animals such as squirrels play an important role in the growth of new trees and plants. The squirrel helps by forgetting some of the acorns, chestnuts, and pinecones it buries. These forgotten nuts and seeds lie dormant in the winter, but then sometimes sprout in the spring. Collect 10 acorns, chestnuts, or small pinecones and hide them in your home or bury them in the ground. Wait a few days; then go back to your spot and try to find the nuts. Can you find them by sight alone? Sniff the ground a little. Does this help you find them? How many of the buried nuts are you able to find?

OPOSSUM

With suction pads on its feet and clawed toes that grip well, an opossum is perfectly suited for climbing. By wrapping its tail around a branch, an opossum can balance high in a tree, away from danger.

What You Need

- White paper
- Poster paint: gray, pink, black, and orange
- Fine black marker

What You Do

1 To print the opossum's body, paint your entire hand gray, leaving your thumb clean, and print in the center of the paper.

2 To form the head, paint a pink leaf shape onto your palm and print so it overlaps the body slightly.

3 Make the pink ears and feet using your pointer fingertip. Print the tail by joining a line of pink fingerprints.

Naturally Speaking

OPOSSUMS ARE MARSUPIALS, WHICH ARE MAMMALS THAT CARRY THEIR YOUNG IN A POUCH. THE OPOSSUM IS THE ONLY MARSUPIAL FOUND IN NORTH AMERICA.

4 Make a little orange nose and a little black eye using fingertip prints.

5 Outline when dry, adding the details to the tail, paws, ears, and nose. Don't forget the whiskers!

DOWN ON THE FARM

SWAN

Swans are closely related to geese, although they are usually much larger. Male swans, called cobs, mate with females, or pens, and live together for their lifetime.

What You Need

🖌 White paper
🖌 Poster paint: white, black, blue, and orange

What You Do

1 Form the blue, watery background using horizontal pointer fingerprints. Let dry.

2 To form the swan's body and tail feathers, paint your hand white and print horizontally on paper with your fingers pointing left and your thumb pointing upward.

3 To form the rest of the swan's white neck, use a pointer fingertip print.

4 To form the swan's black head, use a pointer fingertip print.

5 Print the swan's orange beak using the top section of your pinky. When dry, outline, and add the details to the beak and eye.

Family Ties

Swans feed mostly on water plants and have a jagged-edged bill and a spiny tongue that help pull up plants and tear them apart. Swans feed from the bottom of ponds, using their long, graceful necks for reaching. They have strong family ties, mating for life, as lions, ducks, and people often do. The pair builds the nest, but in most species, only the female incubates the eggs. The male helps to feed and protect the young once they hatch. Baby swans stay with their parents until finding their own mates.

Fold an Origami Swan

Try your hand at origami, the Japanese art of paper-folding. The swan is one of the simpler animals to fold. Follow the illustrations here for a beautiful paper swan.

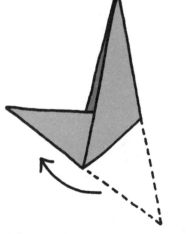

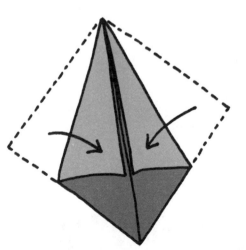

1. Start with a square, fold diagonally. Then fold the sides to the diagonal line.

2. Fold in half, with flaps to the inside. Then fold the bottom-third up and through the inside of the flaps.

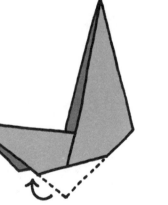

3. Fold the bottom points inward to form the bottom of the swan.

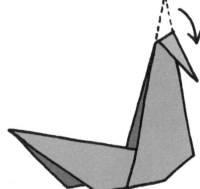

4. Fold the top point downward to form the swan's head. Try coloring your swan a different color besides white.

PIG

ACTIVITY LEVEL

Pigs are actually one of the most intelligent domesticated (tame) animals around. In fact, some are more trainable than horses and dogs!

What You Need

- White paper
- Poster paint: brown and pink
- Fine black marker

What You Do

1 To form the pig's body, paint your palm pink and print onto the center of the paper.

2 Form the pig's ears, nose, and legs, using the top section of your pointer finger.

3 Print some brown mud using your pointer fingertip.

4 Make a curly tail with pink marker. When dry, outline with black marker.

Stupendous Sniffers

Despite popular belief — and appearance! — pigs are very clean animals. Though most pigs live in barnyards, the Vietnamese pot-bellied pig is a popular household pet! Pigs have a keen sense of smell and their hoe-like snouts allow them to root around in the ground for food. In fact, in the forests of the Perigord in southern France, pigs bring in big money by sniffing out delicious truffles, a mushroom delicacy.

Make a Piggy Bank

Save and store coins you've earned or collected in a homemade piggy bank. Ask a grown-up to wash out a small, empty plastic bottle used for bleach or windshield washer fluid and save the bottle cap. With the bottle handle pointed upward, glue four corks or empty thread spools to the bottom of the bottle for legs. Let dry. Ask a grown-up to cut a coin slot in the top about 1 $1/2$" (4 cm) long. Cover the bottle, small areas at a time, with craft glue; then glue on pink tissue paper squares to cover the bottle. Leave the cap end open for a nose. Finger paint eyes and a mouth and glue two small black circles onto the cap for nostrils. Curl a pink pipe cleaner around a pencil for a tail.

ANIMAL ANTICS

Pigs love wallowing in the mud, but it's not because they like being dirty. Wallowing in the mud protects their hairless skin from the sun's heat and from biting insects.

GLUE

COW

Cows have played a role in the daily lives of people for 5,000 to 6,000 years, providing milk, meat, and hides for families around the world.

What You Need

- White paper
- Poster paint: white, black, green, and pink
- Fine black marker

What You Do

1 Form the green, grassy background using vertical pointer fingerprints. Let dry.

2 To print the cow's head, paint a white leaf shape on your palm and print toward the right side of the paper.

3 To form the cow's body, paint your palm white and print.

4 To form the cow's 4 legs and tail, paint the length of your pointer finger white and print.

5 Form the cow's ears with your pointer fingertip dipped in white paint.

6 To form the udders and the nose, dip your pointer fingertip in pink paint and print.

7 To make the cow's spots, hooves, and black areas around the eyes, use black pointer fingertip prints. Print the eyes with small white fingerprints.

8 When dry, outline with marker, adding details to the tail, head, eyes, nose, and landscape.

Texas longhorns are the direct descendants of cattle brought to America from the West Indies by Christopher Columbus. How's that for heritage?

Milk Makers

We rely on cows for everything from butter to sour cream to cream cheese to Swiss cheese. Holstein, Jersey, Guernsey, and Ayrshire cows are great milk producers. Those cows make three to four times as much milk as other cows do. Take a look at a map of the United States and look for Wisconsin, California, New York, and Pennsylvania, the states that have the most dairy cows.

Shake Up Some Butter

Have you ever made butter from a jar of cream? Put 1 cup (250 ml) of heavy cream and 2 tablespoons (25 ml) sour cream in a large, plastic resealable jar and shake, shake, shake it! It will take a while for the butter to form, so you may want to take turns shaking with a friend.

cream and sour cream

butter

Eventually a little lump of butter will form in the cream. Mix this lump with a pinch of salt and spread it on a piece of toast for a tasty, buttery treat!

HORSE

Female horses are called mares, while males are called stallions. Young horses are generally called foals, although male and female foals have special names, too. A colt is a young male and a filly is a young female.

What You Need

- White paper
- Poster paint: brown, black, and green
- Fine black marker

What You Do

1 To form the horse's body, paint your hand brown, leaving your thumb clean, and print with your fingers pointing to the right. Be sure to leave room for the horse's head.

2 To form the neck slanting downward, paint the top 2 sections of your 3 middle fingers brown and print.

3 To print the face, dip your pointer fingertip in brown paint and print twice. Now fingerprint the ear.

4 To form the legs, paint the top 2 sections of your pointer finger brown and print 4 times.

5 To form the black eye, nose, and hooves, use pointer fingertip prints.

6 To make the mane and tail, dip the side of your pinky in black paint and print several times.

7 Make the green grass using the side of your pinky. When dry, outline with a marker.

COOL COLOR OPTION

Horses come in many different colors, some even with spots! Find a book in your local library that has pictures of different kinds of horses; then choose something unusual to print like an Appaloosa or a palomino.

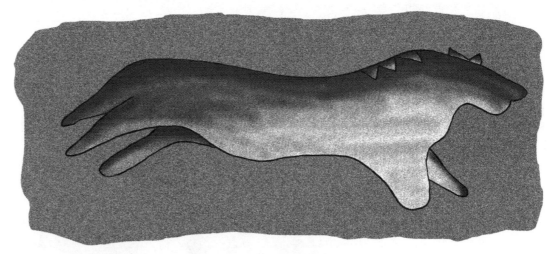

Saddle 'Em Up

Almost since the time people walked the earth, horses frolicked in areas far and wide, from the Middle East to the British Isles. The paintings of horses found in caves in Lascaux, France, are evidence of their connection to humans more than 14,000 years ago. Once they were tamed, horses became "beasts of burden," helping people complete their daily jobs much the way machines do today. As harnesses and other equipment were designed, horses were used for plowing fields, logging forests, transporting royalty, playing polo, and participating in duels and ancient warfare.

Concoct Some Bug Repellent

Horses are bothered by bugs the same way people are, especially during the summer months. Their tails swat away many of the bugs, but horse owners know the secret to keeping biting flies away from large animals is with bug repellent. Here's a recipe a horse would surely thank you for, and best of all, it's all natural and doesn't use ozone-harming aerosol. Mix 1 cup (250 ml) of water with 2 teaspoons (15 ml) of dried chamomile. Ask a grown-up to boil the mixture; then cool and strain before sponging on a horse — or you!

SHEEP

Superstitions about sheep are common among farmers. Supposedly, walking through a flock of sheep brings bad luck. But, if you do happen through a flock and you find a coin in a sheep's track, you'll become rich.

What You Need

- White paper
- Poster paint: white, black, green, and yellow
- Fine black marker

What You Do

1 Form the green, grassy background using vertical pointer fingerprints. Let dry.

2 To form the sheep's body, paint your palm white and print in the center of the paper.

3 To form the sheep's head, paint a small, white leaf shape on the palm of your hand and print.

4 Print the white ear and tail, using your pointer fingertip.

5 Print the sheep's 4 white legs using the top 2 sections of your pointer finger.

6 Print some yellow buttercups in a field using your pointer fingertip.

7 Print the black face of the sheep with your pointer fingertip. Print the white eye with a pinky fingertip print. When dry, outline with marker.

Animals of the Ancients

Scientists believe sheep were among the earliest animals to be raised by Stone Age peoples of western Asia more than 8,000 years ago. They can feed on poor land, and in some places such as New Zealand, there are more sheep than people! Most people raise sheep for their wool and their meat, but some people enjoy sheep as barnyard pets. Wild sheep, like the curly horned species, live in several regions of the world and are large and very timid, not unlike their domesticated cousins. Sheep's milk, mostly in the Mediterranean, is used to make cheese such as Roquefort, but in North America, sheep are most often raised for their wonderfully warm wool.

3-D Sheep Prints

Add a curly coat to your sheep print by cutting white paper into 6" x $^{1}/_{2}$" (15 cm x 2 cm) strips. Wrap each strip tightly around a pencil for curls. Spread a thin layer of craft glue over the sheep's body, and stick the edges of the curls onto the sheep. Let dry. Use different-colored curls of paper, cut at different lengths and widths, for an unusual effect.

DUCK

Many ducks are excellent fliers and migrate, or travel, long distances in the fall and spring. Often, migrating ducks will return to the exact same location year after year to raise ducklings.

What You Need

- White paper
- Poster paint: brown, orange, red, white, blue/green, light blue, and green
- Fine black marker

What You Do

1 To make the duck's body, paint your palm brown and print in the center of the paper.

2 For the tail, paint your 3 middle fingers brown and print.

3 To form the duck's neck, paint the top 2 sections of your pointer finger green/blue and print.

4 To form the duck's head, dip your thumb in green/blue paint and print. Print the white band around the neck using your pinky tip.

5 Just below the band on the neck, make a red thumbprint.

6 To make the duck's legs, paint the top 2 sections of your pointer finger orange and print twice.

7 Print the duck's orange feet using your pointer fingertip. Repeat for the duck's beak and eye.

8 To make a water scene, use lots of small light blue fingerprints.

9 Print some green reeds using the side of your pinky; then put a brown fingerprint on top of each reed.

10 Add details to the tail feathers and the beak and outline if you wish.

Quack! Quack!

The feathers of some male ducks, or drakes, have striking colors and shimmering patterns. The harlequin duck is quite colorful and has a face pattern that makes it appear masked.

Baby ducklings are covered with feathers and can feed themselves and swim right away. Oddly, they have an unusual instinct of following the first moving thing they see upon hatching, be it their mother or not! This funny way of learning is known as "imprinting."

Waddling Duck Relay

All ducks have wide, webbed feet made especially for swimming, which is why ducks waddle when they walk. Borrow a pair of swimming flippers or even a pair of shoes that are a few sizes too big. Invite some friends to bring their flippers or big shoes to join in a waddling relay. Set up a short distance to walk — perhaps from one tree to another — then ready, set, GO! Everyone walks as quickly as possible to the finish and the person who arrives first — with flippers intact — wins!

ANIMAL ANTICS

Ducks spend a lot of time preening themselves, but it's not all about looks. With its broad bill, a duck strokes an oil gland near its tail and then smears the oil all over its feathers to make them waterproof. As they say, it's water off a duck's back!

CHICK

Nearly all countries raise some chickens, but China, Russia, and the United States produce the most.

What You Need

- White paper
- Poster paint: brown, green, yellow, and orange
- Fine black marker

What You Do

1 To make the chick's body, paint your palm yellow and print onto the center of the paper.

2 Print the head using a thumbprint.

3 Print three tail feathers using the top section of your pointer finger dipped in yellow paint.

4 Print an orange beak with the top section of your pinky, and 2 brown legs with the length of your pinky.

5 Make some green grass using the length of your pinky.

6 When dry, outline with marker.

PETS OF ALL KINDS

IGUANA

Iguanas are fast becoming popular pets, partly because they are quiet and fairly easy to care for.

What You Need

- White paper
- Poster paint: light and dark green
- Fine black marker

What You Do

1 To form the iguana's head, paint a light green leaf shape on your palm and print in the top left corner of your paper.

2 To form the skin beneath the chin, dip your thumb in light green paint and print.

3 Print 4 tail sections, leaving a space between each, using the top 2 sections of your pointer finger painted light green.

4 Print the first 4 tail sections, between the light green prints, using the top 2 sections of your pointer finger painted dark green.

Sun Lovers

5 Continue the same pattern, making the prints smaller as you get close to the end of the tail. Print 7 light green sections and 7 dark green sections using your pointer fingertip.

6 Form the larger spikes beneath the iguana's chin and along its back by printing with the side of your pinky.

7 Print the first 2 sections of the iguana's green legs using the top 2 sections of your pointer finger. Print the foot using a pointer fingertip print.

8 When dry, outline with a marker. Draw an eye, a nose, and some spikes on the head and tail.

Iguanas are lizards that originated in the American tropics. Marine iguanas live close to rivers and streams in the Galapagos Islands off the coast of Equador and feed on algae, while land iguanas like to eat plants, including cacti, small animals, insects, and birds. Iguanas are sun lovers and are often seen lounging on rocks or pavement, soaking up the warmth. Iguanas can reach 5 feet (1.5 meters) in length and are bright green when young, but turn a duller green as they age.

Sculpt an Iguana

Mix together 1 1/2 cups (375 ml) salt, 4 cups (1 l) flour, and 1 1/2 cups (375 ml) water. Knead well, adding extra water if the mixture is too crumbly. Sculpt an iguana shape from the clay, and ask a grown-up to bake it at 300°F (150°C) for 20 to 30 minutes. (The thicker your iguana, the longer it needs to bake.) Once it has cooled, paint it bright green and add details to its face and body. Attach to a piece of bark or a branch for a realistic sculpture.

GUINEA PIG

Guinea pigs aren't really pigs, of course. They're closely related to mice and other rodents. Their name may have arisen from the soft squeaking or grunting piglike noises they make.

What You Need

- White paper
- Poster paint: brown, gray, pink, white, and green
- Fine black marker

What You Do

1 To form the body, paint your hand with brown and gray patches, but leave your thumb clean. Print in the center of your paper.

2 Print the 2 brown legs and an ear, using your pointer fingertip.

3 Print the white eye using your pointer fingertip. Print a pink nose using a fingerprint.

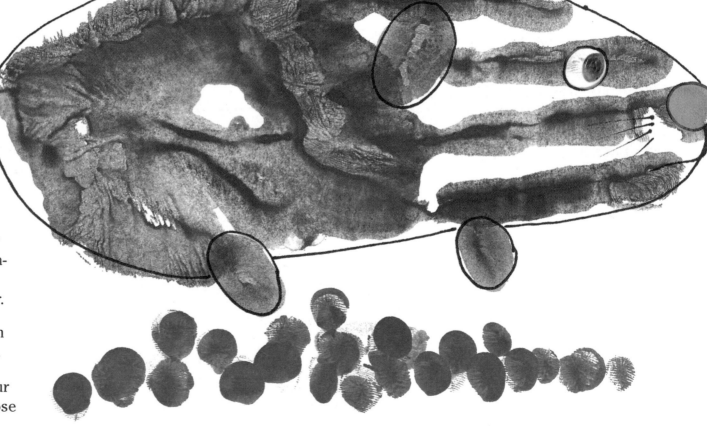

4 Print the grass with green fingerprints.

5 When dry, outline, and draw some whiskers.

Furry Friends

Guinea pigs make excellent pets. Once they become used to their surroundings, they like being held and become very tame. Domesticated guinea pigs come in a variety of colors, but wild ones are only black and gray. Wild guinea pigs still live in the grasslands of South America, where they stay close together in groups and live in burrows.

Eat a Vegetarian Meal

Guinea pigs are vegetarians, which means they eat only vegetables, seeds, fruits, and nuts. You may know some people who are vegetarians, too. If you eat red meat, chicken, and fish, why not spend one meal eating as a vegetarian would? It's fun to eat new foods — and who knows, you may even

awaken some new taste sensations. Guinea pigs enjoy carrots, cauliflower, broccoli, cabbage, celery, and apples. Arrange some samples of these foods on a plate and nibble away. Dip your snacks in a bit of salad dressing for a zippy treat.

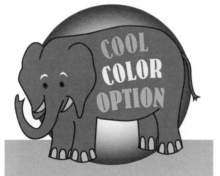

COOL COLOR OPTION

Guinea pigs come in shades of tan, white, black, brown, and other light colors. Try these colors out and mix two of them together for two-toned guinea pigs.

GOLDFISH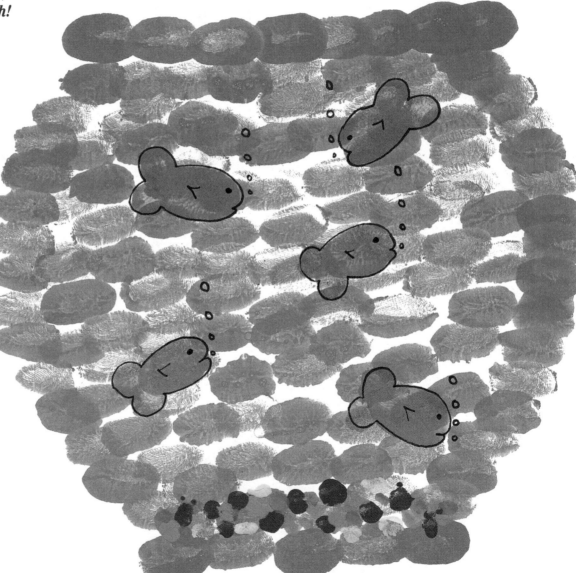

Goldfish adapt their size to their environment. In fish bowls, they grow to only a few inches, but in the wild, they can be up to a foot in length!

What You Need

- White paper
- Poster paint: orange, blue, yellow, red, green, and purple
- Fine black marker

What You Do

1. Form the fishbowl shape using horizontal fingertip prints. Let dry.

2. Print a few orange goldfish in the bowl, using your thumbprints.

3. Form the tails for each fish using 2 pinky fingertip prints.

4. Print the rocks at the bottom of the bowl, using your pointer fingertip dipped in each of the colors.

5. When dry, outline, adding fins, eyes, mouths, and bubbles.

Peaceful Pets

Domesticated goldfish originated in China and belong to the family of fish called carp. Goldfish are peaceful fish and are easy to feed and keep as pets. Some goldfish have lived to be 30 and 40 years old. In Japan, people fly silk kites and windsocks in an annual kite-flying festival. Perhaps the most outstanding designs seen on the kites are those of bright-colored fish.

Make a Paper Bag Windsock

On each side of a small paper bag, make a colorful fish design using glitter and glue, crayons, or paint. Cut the bottom off the bag and make a ring of poster board to fit exactly into the top of the bag at the end with the fish's head. Glue the ring in place and let dry, or use a stapler or paper clips to hold in place. Make a hole through the ring and tie a 12-inch (30 cm) length of string to it. Tie the other end to a dowel or stick. Glue on colorful tissue paper or colored paper strips to the opposite end of the bag for a fish tail. Hold the dowel and wave your hand-held windsock in the air.

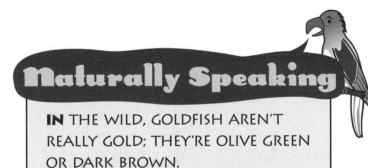

Naturally Speaking

IN THE WILD, GOLDFISH AREN'T REALLY GOLD; THEY'RE OLIVE GREEN OR DARK BROWN.

RABBIT

The Flemish giant rabbit can grow to be 15 pounds (7 kg) — the size of a small dog!

What You Need

- White paper
- Poster paint: white, orange, green, and pastel colors
- Fine black marker

What You Do

1. To form the body, paint your left hand in pastel-colored blotches and print onto paper with your thumb pointing upward to form the ear.

2. Fingerprint a tail, a pink nose and a white eye, using pointer fingertips.

3. Form the pastel-colored back leg using 2 sections of your pointer finger. Use a pointer fingerprint for the front leg.

4. Print an orange carrot using the length of your pointer finger. To form the greens, use your pinky tip dipped in green. Outline when dry.

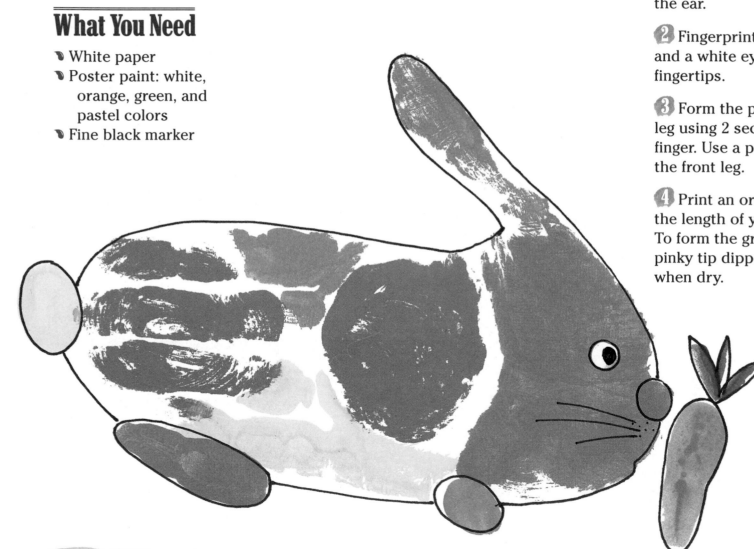

Rabbit or Hare ?

Rabbits and hares are similar in appearance, but they are different in some ways, too. Baby rabbits are born hairless, blind, and helpless, but hares are born furry and open-eyed, ready to hop around right away. Hares also give birth on the ground in a small, hollowed area, not underground as some rabbits do. Hares run from danger, but rabbits are more likely to hide in burrows that they dig themselves.

Rabbits live all over the world except in Antarctica, and are known for producing lots of babies. In the wild, a female rabbit can have as many as seven litters of four to six babies — as many as 42 babies per year! Rabbits are well-equipped for life in the wild. They have long ears for good hearing, an excellent sense of smell, and beautiful, oily coats that keep cold rain and snow away from their skin.

See How a Rabbit's Coat Keeps It Dry

Many animals, including labrador retrievers, beavers, and ducks, rely on their oily coats to help keep them dry and warm when they're in the water. Their oily coats work so well because water and oil are immiscible, which means they won't mix. See for yourself by pouring $1/4$ cup (55 ml) vegetable oil into a jar that contains $1/2$ cup (125 ml) water. Cover the jar and shake; then watch what happens as the two liquids settle. They just won't mix, will they?

CAT

Cats have been around for centuries. In fact, ancient Egyptians worshipped the cat and treated it as a sacred animal as early as 3000 B.C.

What You Need

- White paper
- Poster paint: brown and blue
- Fine black marker

What You Do

1 To form the body, paint your palm in spots, using all the colors except blue, and print onto paper.

2 Repeat the process for the head and print, overlapping the body slightly.

3 Form the cat's ears using 2 fingerprints.

4 Print the cat's tail and front legs using the length of your pointer finger.

5 Fingerprint a blue ball of yarn between the 2 front paws.

6 Fingerprint a small black nose and 2 small white eyes.

7 Finish your cat's eyes, using a marker. When dry, outline, and draw whiskers and a mouth.

Those Darn Cats

Domestic cats evolved as urban scavengers. In the year 8000 B.C., cats began living closer to humans until they were eventually kept as companions. All cats, large and small, behave similarly, putting ears back, moving their tails, and hissing to warn animals that threaten them. They've also been known to scratch trees (and sofas!) to stretch their limbs. Perhaps the best-known cats are those you may have read about. Are you familiar with the Cheshire cat of *Alice in Wonderland*, the *Cat in the Hat*, and Felix?

Grow Some Catnip

There's an herb called "catnip" that cats go wild for. They lick it, they roll in it, and they eat it! You can grow your own catnip for a special cat without much trouble. Just purchase catnip seeds from a garden supply store and follow package directions for planting. Or, purchase seedlings and plant either outside or in a container placed in a sunny window. Once the plants begin to mature, they're guaranteed to attract plenty of attention from your favorite feline.

DOG

Dogs belong to a family of animals called canids, also known as canines. Wild dogs, like wolves, dingoes, red foxes, and coyotes, are cousins of the dogs we enjoy as pets.

What You Need

- White paper
- Poster paint: golden brown, black, pink, and red
- Fine black marker

What You Do

1 To form your dog's head, paint your hand golden brown, and print. Your pinky will form the dog's lower jaw and your thumb will form one ear.

2 To form the body, paint your palm golden brown and print.

3 Fingerprint the pink tongue, a black nose, and a white eye.

4 To print the other ear, use the length of your pointer finger. Repeat for the red collar.

5 When dry, outline, and draw whiskers and an eye.

Dogs at Work

Many dogs are bred to look and behave in certain ways or to perform certain jobs. German shepherds are used in the armed forces for security, while border collies are kept on farms for herding animals. Many dogs are bred so their bodies are suited for certain purposes, be it for hunting (basset hound), herding (sheep dog), racing (greyhound), or Seeing-Eye (retriever). A greyhound is built for speed with its lean body, long muscular legs, and streamlined body. Basset hounds have long, sensitive noses for sniffing game and short legs so owners can keep up with them while hunting.

Bake Dog Biscuits

Here's a treat any dog will love! Combine 1 cup (250 ml) rolled oats, $1/3$ cup (75 ml) butter, and 1 cup (250 ml) boiling water (ask for grown-up help) and let stand 10 minutes. Stir in $3/4$ cup (175 ml) cornmeal, 1 tablespoon (15 ml) of sugar, and 1-2 teaspoons (5-10 ml) of chicken broth. Add $1/2$ cup (125 ml) milk, 1 cup (250 ml) shredded cheddar cheese, and 1 beaten egg. Mix well. Add 2 $1/2$ cups (625 ml) of flour, one cup at a time, mixing well to form a stiff dough. Knead the dough for a few minutes; then roll or pat it down to $1/2$" (1 cm) thickness. Cut with a bone-shaped cookie cutter and place on greased cookie sheets. Ask a grown-up to cook the biscuits in a 325°F (160°C) oven for 35-45 minutes.

TARANTULA

The Latin name for tarantula is aranas peludas, which means "the hairy spiders."

What You Need

❥ White paper
❥ Poster paint: black and white

What You Do

1 To make the body, paint your palm black and print onto paper. To form the tarantula's head, paint a smaller circle on your palm and overlap the body slightly.

2 Give the tarantula 8 legs using the length of your longest finger dipped in paint.

3 Make the tarantula's mouth using black fingerprints.

4 For the eyes, use white finger-prints.

Step Into My Underground Parlor

Contrary to popular belief, tarantulas are not poisonous to humans. Their bites, however, like the sting of a bee, can cause allergic reactions in people who are sensitive to insect bites. Tarantulas can live to be 20 years old and are often kept as pets. In the wild, tarantulas must be on the lookout for skunk, wild pig, and coatimundi (a small mammal related to raccoons), which like dining on the hairy spiders. Tarantulas live in burrows and do not spin webs as other spiders do. Instead, they trap prey by creating trap doors, silken trap doormats, or mounds of grass at the entrance to their burrows.

Make a Web Print

Find an abandoned or vacant spider web hanging in an open space. Be sure not to disturb any webs with spiders in or around them. Blow talcum powder over the web in a fine even layer. Spread a thin layer of glue over a piece of black cardboard and place it behind the web. Gently attach the web to the card without changing its shape. Push the cardboard against the web and cut away the threads anchoring it. Ask a grown-up to spray the web with a light coat of varnish and let dry.

The bird-eating tarantula of South America can grow to be as big as your dinner plate!

HAMSTER

Hamsters are known for hoarding food, which they collect in pouches in their cheeks.

What You Need

- White paper
- Poster paint: yellow/tan and pink
- Fine black marker

What You Do

1. To form the hamster's head, paint a leaf shape on your palm and print close to the right side of the paper.

2. To paint the body, paint your palm and print, overlapping the head slightly.

3. To form the hamster's ear, tail, and legs, dip your pointer finger in the tan paint and print.

4. Make a little pink nose using a pink fingerprint.

5. When dry, outline with a marker, and add an eye, a mouth, a tooth, and some whiskers.

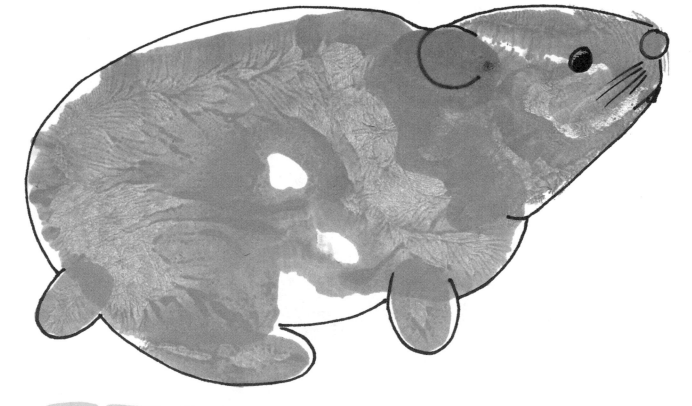

Funny Fact

One farmer found nearly 100 pounds (45 kg) of grain in a wild hamster's burrow!

ANIMALS FROM NEAR & FAR

POLAR BEAR

Polar bears are 6 to 8 feet (1.8 to 2.4 m) long — twice the size of a lion or tiger — and can weigh as much as an automobile!

What You Need

- White paper
- Poster paint: white, black, and blue
- Fine black marker

What You Do

1 Form an icy, blue background using horizontal pointer fingerprints. Let dry.

2 To form the polar bear's body, paint your right hand and the first section of your thumb white and place your fingers so they face the left side of your page. Print.

3 To form the face of your polar bear, paint the top 2 sections of your 3 middle fingers and print.

4 Make the polar bear's ear using a white fingertip print.

5 Print the white front leg, using the top 2 sections of your pointer finger. Print the paws of the front and back legs using white fingerprints.

6 When dry, outline, and add details to the paws with a marker.

Look At My Fur

A polar bear's fur serves as both a sun collector and as great camouflage for hunting prey in the treeless, icy arctic. Its hairs, which are tiny see-through "tubes," trap ultraviolet light and lead it to the bear's black skin. Because the color black absorbs energy from the sun, the polar bear's coat soaks up the sun, keeping the bear warm.

Feel the Heat

Some homes are heated with solar energy, or warmth from the sun. The sun's warmth keeps us warm, too. Have you ever noticed that on a sunny day, dark clothes make you feel hotter? Just like the polar bear's black skin, a black shirt will absorb more heat than a white shirt (which reflects it). Try this experiment on a sunny day: Fill two jars halfway with cold water. Put the lids back on. Wrap one jar with black construction paper and the other jar with white paper. Place the jars outside in a sunny spot; then check the water an hour later. Which jar's water is warmer?

ANIMAL ANTICS

Polar bears have been known to stray 750 miles (1,200 km) south of their Arctic Circle home to raid garbage dumps and landfills. Ick!

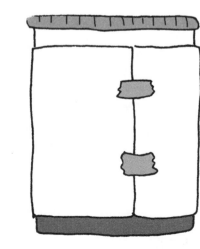
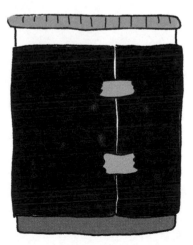

KOALA BEAR

(ACTIVITY LEVEL)

Koalas aren't true bears like black and brown bears (see page 72) — they're marsupials, or animals that carry their young in a fur pouch on their bellies.

What You Need

- White paper
- Poster paint: light and dark brown, light and dark gray, black, pink, green, and red
- Fine black marker

What You Do

1 To form the koala's face, paint your palm light brown and print in the center of the paper.

2 Use thumbprints to form the light gray ears and the area around the eyes. Thumbprint a dark gray nose.

3 To form the end of the koala's nose, dip your pointer fingertip in pink paint and print.

4 To form a twig, dip the side of your pinky in dark brown paint and print, joining together the little prints. Add green leaves to the branch using pointer fingerprints.

5 Make the fur on the top and bottom of the ears by dipping the side of your pinky tip in black paint and printing over and over.

6 Form the fur on the sides of the face by dipping the side of your pinky tip in light gray paint and printing.

7 Print red eyes with your pointer fingertip.

8 When dry, add details to the koala's eyes, nose, mouth, and fur on his ears and cheeks. Add veins to the leaves.

The word koala comes from the Australian aborigine word meaning, "no drink." Can you see why that is?

Eucalyptus—Tree of Life

K oalas live only in the eucalyptus forests of Eastern Australia, where they are protected by law. Despite efforts to protect koalas, they are still threatened by the destruction of eucalyptus forests for development. Eucalyptus trees are the koalas' main food and water source. Amazingly, koalas rarely drink water. They receive all the liquids they need from the leaves of — you guessed it — the eucalyptus tree.

Eucalyptus Potpourri

Perhaps the koala likes eucalyptus so much because it smells so good! There are many other plants that have wonderful scents and can be used to make potpourri. Gather together some dried eucalyptus or use dry rose petals and lavender blossoms. Add peppermint leaves, lemon, lime, or orange peel (available from health food, grocery, or craft store). Place on a tea towel and microwave for 3-5 minutes until dry like autumn leaves when cooled. Mix several cups of dried flowers or peel

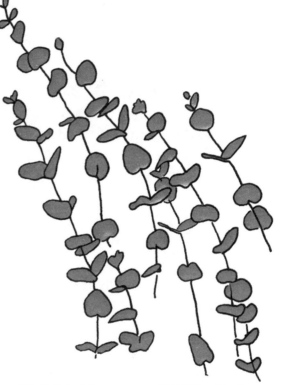

with 1-2 tablespoons (15-30 ml) cinnamon, nutmeg, cloves, or ginger. Add 6-10 drops of lemon, orange, or rose oil and 2 teaspoons (10 ml) of orrisroot (from health food or grocery store) and mix again. Place in tiny baskets or boxes to add a fresh scent to a drawer or room.

KANGAROO

There are 50 different species of kangaroo living in Tasmania, Australia, New Guinea, and New Zealand. When people talk about large groups of kangaroos, they call them mobs!

What You Need

- White paper
- Poster paint: light and dark gray, black
- Fine black marker

What You Do

1 To form the kangaroo body, paint your palm light gray and print.

2 To print the head, paint the top 2 sections of your 3 middle fingers light gray, and with your fingertips pointing toward the kangaroo's body, print on the paper.

3 To form the kangaroo's thighs, dip your thumbtip in light gray paint and print.

4 To form the kangaroo's legs and arms, paint the top 2 sections of your pointer finger light gray and print.

5 For the adult kangaroo's feet, lower arms and ears, use a light gray fingerprint. Form the tail by joining lots of light gray finger-prints.

6 Print the joey's dark gray head between the mother kangaroo's hands using your pointer fingertip.

7 Form the joey's dark gray ears with pinky fingertip prints.

8 Print the kangaroo's black ears and eyes and the joey's black ears using your pointer fingertip.

9 Print the kangaroo's black nose and the joey's black eye and nose with your pinky fingertip.

10 When dry, outline and add details to the kangaroo's face, hands, feet, and eyes. Then, add details to the joey.

High Jumpers

Kangaroos are marsupials with a large pouch for young (called joeys) to grow and nurse in for up to eight months. Only female kangas have pouches. Kangaroos have large hind legs for jumping, small front legs, and a strong muscular tail that helps them balance. They can run for short distances at 30 mph (48 km/h), and when moving at high speeds can jump 30 feet (9 m) high.

Jump Up High

People can't jump as high as kangaroos, of course, but Dick Fosbury of the U.S. jumped as high as any human in history at the 1968 Olympics — a record 7 feet 4 $1/2$ inches (2.21 m)! To see how high you can jump, ask 2 friends to hold a piece of string a short height off the ground. Measure the height of the string with a yardstick before each jump; then jump over the string. Once you have cleared the string, have the string held a little higher until you can jump no higher. Now let your friends have a turn. Who is able to jump the highest?

TIGER

Believe it or not, only about 150-200 Siberian tigers remain in the wild. In all, there are only about 4,700 tigers living in the wild areas of China, Sumatra, India, and Siberia today.

What You Need

🖌 White paper
🖌 Poster paint: orange, black, white, and brown
🖌 Fine black marker

What You Do

1 To form the tiger's face, paint your palm orange and print in the center of your paper.

2 To form the tiger's ears, dip your thumbtip into orange paint and print.

3 Print the white markings around the eyes, on the chin and cheeks, and in the center of the ears with thumbprints.

4 Print the tiger's markings using the side of your longest finger painted black and the side of your pinky painted black.

5 Form a brown nose using a thumbprint.

6 When dry, outline, and add details to the eyes, nose, mouth, top lip, and whiskers.

Disappearing Act

Tigers are the largest, most powerful members of the cat family. They live in the cold wastelands of Manchuria and Siberia, the thorn bushes of India, and the hot, bamboo jungles and rain forests of Malaysia. Sadly, these beautiful animals have been hunted heavily and had their forest habitat cleared in South Asia, where they have disappeared completely. Siberian and Sumatran tigers are close to extinction in the wild, but you can still see tigers in wildlife preserves and zoos around the country.

Hiding Out

A tiger's striped coat helps to camouflage or hide it from its prey. Print your striped tiger on a piece of sand-colored construction paper; then surround it with grass cuttings and hay for a 3-D camouflage print. How well can you hide the tiger?

ZEBRA

Just as each snowflake is unique to the world, no two zebras have the same arrangement of stripes. In fact, most recognize one another based on their unique stripe arrangements.

What You Need

- White paper
- Poster paint: black
- Fine black marker

What You Do

1 To form the body, paint black stripes across your right hand, leaving your thumb clean; then print onto paper with your fingers pointing to the left.

2 To form the neck and head, paint black stripes on your 4 fingers and print at an angle.

3 To form the zebra's legs, paint black stripes on your longest finger and print.

4 To form the zebra's tail, paint black stripes on your pointer finger and print.

5 Print the zebra's nose using a black thumbtip print. Use a black pointer fingertip print for the eye, ear, and hooves.

6 When dry, outline, and add some tassels to the end of the tail.

Ponies in Pajamas

Zebras are members of the horse family and have dark brown or black stripes, which camouflage them from predators in the savannah and dry scrub areas where they live. From a distance, their striped bodies blend with the mirages caused by intense heat in the bush. Zebras can be found from Ethiopia to South Africa in steadily decreasing numbers, due to hunting for their skins.

Black & White Collage

Collect black and white pictures, newspaper, photos, buttons, fabric, and beads for a zebra-striped collage. Look for magazine pictures of people in black and white clothing, black and white cars, black and white dishes, appliances, and flowers. Now, draw or trace the outline of a horse, pony, or zebra from a magazine or book; then use your cutouts to make the zebra's stripes.

ANIMAL ANTICS

Zebras communicate silently with each other and alert other zebras to nearby danger by moving their large ears this way and that.

CAMEL

ACTIVITY LEVEL

A camel's hump stores fat, not water as some people believe. As the camel's fat reserves are used up, the humps begin to shrink and sag.

What You Need

❧ White paper
❧ Poster paint: brown, tan, dark blue, and black
❧ Fine black marker

What You Do

1 To form the camel's body, paint your palm brown and print in the center of the paper.

2 To form the camel's tail and 2 front legs, paint the length of your pointer finger brown and print.

3 To form the top and bottom parts of the camel's back legs, paint the top 2 sections of your pointer finger brown and print.

4 For the humps, dip your thumbtip in the brown paint and print.

5 Make the camel's curved neck using thumbprints joined in line; then form the head using a thumbprint.

6 Form an ear using your pointer fingertip dipped in brown paint.

7 Make the eye with a dark blue fingertip and the nose with a black fingerprint.

8 Print the tan rocks and sand using your pinky fingertip and pointer fingertip.

9 When dry, outline, and add details to the nose, mouth, eye, ear, and tail.

Funny Fact

In the mid 1800s, the U.S. Army brought camels into the United States to carry cargo from Texas to California. The camels escaped and lived in the wild in the Arizona desert until 1905!

One Hump or Two?

The one-humped camel, called the dromedary, was domesticated more than 500 years ago in desert regions of the Middle East. It has provided transport, milk, meat, wool, hides, and dried manure for fuel to the people in that area of the world for hundreds of years. The two-humped camel, the bactrian, is more docile and was domesticated 2,500 years ago. Both camels are well-adapted to desert life with their padded feet, which are good for walking on sand. Their large eyelashes are helpful also in protecting their eyes during sandstorms. Camels get the water they need from desert vegetation, and can survive for months without actually drinking.

Make a Camel Caravan

Handprint a whole bunch of camels onto poster board, cut them out, and join them into a caravan (a train of animals) by gluing on brightly colored yarn. Braid or twist the yarn and use bright-colored fabrics to decorate the camels. Fray the fabric and drape over the camels for a blanket. Use ribbon or braided yarn for camel harnesses.

LION

Lions used to be common in Europe, Africa, and Asia. Today they are only found in protected areas south of the Sahara in Africa and in the Gir Forest, a wildlife sanctuary in India. They are often used as symbols of beauty, power, and courage.

What You Need

- White paper
- Poster paint: tan, orange, light and dark brown
- Fine black marker

What You Do

1 To form the lion's face and mane, paint your entire hand with tan paint and print in the center of your page. Your palm will form the head, your fingers will be part of the mane.

2 Form the rest of the mane using the other colors and the length of your fingers.

3 Give your lion 2 brown ears and a nose using your pointer finger prints.

4 Form the lion's white eyes using fingerprints.

5 When dry, draw the pupils in the eyes, the whiskers, a mouth, and teeth, and outline the ears.

King of the Beasts

While most people believe the male lion is the center of the lion family, or pride, it is actually the female who does most of the hunting for the family. Lions hunt at night and help keep the population of grazing animals in balance in the open, grassy plains and thorn bush country, where they live. Prides of lions are very territorial and don't allow lions from other prides near their land. When they do come too close, you can be sure a fight will soon follow. A lion's mane makes the cat look larger and more frightening to other large animals, and it serves to protect the lion while fighting.

3-D Lion's Mane

Print the face of your lion, without the mane, onto the back of an old greeting card. Then, hole punch circles all around the lion's face. Use a blunt-ended knitting needle with yellow, orange, and brown yarn to "sew" loops randomly around the face for a shaggy mane. Go in and out of each hole a few times using different colors. Leave the yarn loopy for a fuller mane. Or, thread narrow strips of colored fabric through the holes and tie them. Cut the strips with pinking shears for an extra shaggy mane.

ALLIGATOR

Alligators belong to a class of animals called reptiles, which are cold-blooded, egg-laying vertebrates that breathe air and crawl on their short legs or bellies.

What You Need

- White paper
- Poster paint: green and black
- Fine black marker

What You Do

1 Paint palm, pointer, and middle fingers green. Print with 2 fingers separated to form the jaws and head, facing to the right side of the page.

2 To form the body, repaint palm green and print next to the head. Repeat for the rear of the alligator.

3 To form the green tail, continue printing with your palm, each time covering a narrower area.

4 To form the end of the tail use 3, then 2, then 1 pointer fingerprint.

5 Print the rear leg using thumbprints, and the front leg using 2 sections of your pointer finger.

6 Fingerprint a black eye and a nostril. Add teeth and outline the alligator with a fine black marker.

Alligator or Crocodile?

Alligators are related to crocodiles, but they are different in many ways. Alligators have broad, rounded snouts and lack the exposed fourth tooth of the upper jaw seen on crocodiles. They live in lakes, swamps, and slow-moving streams in the eastern US coastal plains, from North Carolina to Florida to Texas. They like to eat insects, crayfish, minnows, frogs, large fish, water birds, turtles, and small mammals. Once in danger of extinction from hunters, the alligator has made a strong comeback, due in part to the protection they received as an endangered species.

Make a Scaly Alligator

Handprint your alligator and let it dry completely. Then, cover the entire print with a layer of craft glue. Sprinkle crushed eggshells (from hard-boiled eggs) over the glue and press down to flatten. Add a few tooth-shaped eggshells to the jaws after painting. Let dry. Finish by painting the alligator a grayish green, adding details to its eye using a marker.

ANIMAL ANTICS

As soon as the young alligators hatch, they call out for their mother who responds to their calls immediately. She leads them to water or will carry them in her mouth.

GIRAFFE

Giraffes always look like they're eating because they chew their cuds, or ruminate, just like cows, sheep, goats, and camels do.

What You Need

- White paper
- Poster paint: gold, brown, and tan
- Fine black marker

What You Do

1 Print the body in the center of the paper, using your palm and gold paint. Print the rear and chest of the giraffe using your palm and gold paint.

2 Form the base of the neck and thighs using a thumbtip print.

3 Use middle fingertip prints to form the legs and upper neck.

4 Print the face and nose, using a pointer fingertip. Print the tail using your entire pinky.

5 Form the tail with a gold pinky tip print. Form the mane and ear with tan pointer fingerprints.

6 Form the horn with a brown pinky tip print. Fingerprint brown spots.

7 Form the eye and end of tail with pinky tip prints. Outline when dry.

Watching Watchtowers

The giraffe is the tallest living animal on earth. With its long legs and neck, it can tower as tall as 18 feet (5.5 m). Amazingly, while standing it can observe animals a mile away. The patterns on the giraffe's skin help camouflage it while it stands in the shade of trees. Giraffes live on the tree-dotted grasslands south of the Sahara in Africa and feed on acacia and mimosa leaves. Their long necks and tongues allow them to reach the highest branches for the leaves.

Walk on Homemade Stilts

Imagine being a walking watchtower yourself! Have you seen the clowns in circuses and carnivals walking on stilts? Using two empty coffee cans and some heavy string, you can make some stilts and see what it's like to be a little taller. Ask a grown-up to make holes in each side of the coffee cans; then you thread the string through, long enough for you to hold while standing atop the cans. Practice walking on a grassy surface to avoid falling down.

Funny Fact

Giraffes are very observant creatures. One giraffe handler in the San Diego Zoo found out just how much when he placed a thumbtack on the wall of the giraffes' dimly lit stall while they were feeding in the yard. When he opened the stall door to let them in, they stuck their heads in, spotted the tack, and refused to enter until the thumbtack was removed!

ELEPHANT

The elephant's trunk is really an elongated nose! It has two nostrils and one or two fingerlike projections for the elephant to use to examine or grasp objects.

What You Need

❥ White paper
❥ Poster paint: light and dark gray, black, and white
❥ Fine black marker

What You Do

1 To form the elephant's body, paint your palm light gray and print in the center of your paper.

2 To form the head, paint a light gray circle in the center of your palm and print, overlapping the body slightly.

3 For the elephant's ears, paint a light gray leaf shape on your palm and print.

4 To make the elephant's legs, paint your tallest finger light gray and print. Use a light gray thumbprint for the feet.

5 For the elephant's tusks, dip the side of your pinky in white paint and print, bending your pinky slightly. Form the trunk by joining lots of dark gray finger-prints.

6 Fingerprint 2 black eyes.

7 When dry, outline and add details to the eyes, trunk, and feet.

COOL COLOR OPTION

Give your elephant a new "wardrobe" by dressing it with dark or bright colors that would help it blend into a rain-forest.

Mammoth Mammal

The African elephant is the largest living land animal, weighing in at 16,500 pounds (7,500 kg), about the size of 4 compact cars put together. Elephants drink by sucking water into their trunks and then squirting it into their mouths. Both female and male African elephants have tusks. Sadly, elephants are endangered because poachers (people who hunt animals illegally) kill them for their beautiful and valuable ivory tusks.

Enough to Feed an Elephant

An adult elephant eats as much as 500 pounds (230 kg) of plant material each day! If a head of lettuce weighs about 2 pounds (1 kg), how many heads of lettuce would you need to feed an elephant each day? Next time you're at the grocery store, check the price of lettuce. How much would an elephant cost to feed for one day?

INDEX

MORE GOOD BOOKS FROM WILLIAMSON PUBLISHING

Kids Can!®

The following Kids Can! books for ages 4 to 10 are each 160-178 pages, fully illustrated, trade paper, 11 x 8 ½, $12.95 US.

CUT-PAPER PLAY!
Dazzling Creations from Construction Paper
  by Sandi Henry

Early Childhood News Directors' Choice Award
VROOM! VROOM!
Making 'dozers, 'copters, trucks & more
  by Judy Press

BOREDOM BUSTERS!
The Curious Kids' Activity Book
  by Avery Hart & Paul Mantell

COOL CRAFTS & AWESOME ART!
A Kids' Treasure Trove of Fabulous Fun
  by Roberta Gould

Oppenheim Toy Portfolio Best Book Award
American Bookseller Pick of the Lists
Benjamin Franklin Best Nonfiction Award
SUPER SCIENCE CONCOCTIONS
50 Mysterious Mixtures for Fabulous Fun
  by Jill Frankel Hauser

Dr. Toy Best Vacation Product
Parents' Choice Gold Award
Parents Magazine Parents' Pick
THE KIDS' NATURE BOOK *(Newly Revised)*
365 Indoor/Outdoor Activities and Experiences
  by Susan Milord

Benjamin Franklin Best Multicultural Book Award
Parents' Choice Approved
Skipping Stones Multicultural Honor Award
THE KIDS' MULTICULTURAL COOKBOOK
Food & Fun Around the World
  by Deanna F. Cook

KIDS' COMPUTER CREATIONS
Using Your Computer for Art & Craft Fun
  by Carol Sabbeth

Parents' Choice Approved
Dr. Toy Best Vacation Product Award
KIDS GARDEN!
The Anytime, Anyplace Guide to Sowing & Growing Fun
  by Avery Hart and Paul Mantell

Winner of the Oppenheim Toy Portfolio Best Book Award
American Bookseller Pick of the Lists
THE KIDS' SCIENCE BOOK
Creative Experiences for Hands-On Fun
  by Robert Hirschfeld and Nancy White

Parents' Choice Gold Award
American Bookseller Pick of the Lists
Winner of the Oppenheim Toy Portfolio Best Book Award
THE KIDS' MULTICULTURAL ART BOOK
Art & Craft Experiences from Around the World
  by Alexandra M. Terzian

Parents' Choice Gold Award
Benjamin Franklin Best Juvenile Nonfiction Award
KIDS MAKE MUSIC!
Clapping and Tapping from Bach to Rock
  by Avery Hart and Paul Mantell

American Bookseller Pick of the Lists
KIDS' CRAZY CONCOCTIONS
50 Mysterious Mixtures for Art & Craft Fun
  by Jill Frankel Hauser

Winner of the Oppenheim Toy Portfolio Best Book Award
Skipping Stones Nature & Ecology Honor Award
EcoArt!
Earth-Friendly Art & Craft Experiences for 3- to 9-Year-Olds
  by Laurie Carlson

KIDS COOK!
Fabulous Food for the Whole Family
  by Sarah Williamson and Zachary Williamson

THE KIDS' WILDLIFE BOOK
Exploring Animal Worlds through Indoor/Outdoor
Crafts & Experiences
  by Warner Shedd

HANDS AROUND THE WORLD
365 Creative Ways to Build Cultural Awareness & Global Respect
  by Susan Milord

KIDS CREATE!
Art & Craft Experiences for 3- to 9-Year-Olds
  by Laurie Carlson

Parents Magazine Parents' Pick
KIDS LEARN AMERICA!
Bringing Geography to Life with People, Places, & History
  by Patricia Gordon and Reed C. Snow

American Bookseller Pick of the Lists
ADVENTURES IN ART *(Newly Revised)*
Art & Craft Experiences for 8- to 13-Year-Olds
  by Susan Milord

Little Hands™

The following *Little Hands*™ books for ages 2 to 6 are each 144 pages, fully illustrated, trade paper, 10 x 8, $12.95 US.

MATH PLAY!
80 Ways to Count & Learn
  by Diane McGowan and Mark Schrooten

American Bookseller Pick of the Lists
RAINY DAY PLAY!
Explore, Create, Discover, Pretend
  by Nancy Fusco Castaldo

Parents' Choice Gold Award
FUN WITH MY 5 SENSES
Activities to Build Learning Readiness
  by Sarah A. Williamson

Children's BOMC Main Selection
THE LITTLE HANDS ART BOOK
Exploring Arts & Crafts with 2- to 6-Year-Olds
  by Judy Press

Parents' Choice Approved
Early Childhood News Directors' Choice Award
SHAPES, SIZES, & MORE SURPRISES!
A Little Hands Early Learning Book
  by Mary Tomczyk

Parents' Choice Approved
The Little Hands BIG FUN CRAFT Book
Creative Fun for 2- to 6-Year-Olds
  by Judy Press

Parents' Choice Approved
THE LITTLE HANDS NATURE BOOK
Earth, Sky, Critters & More
  by Nancy Fusco Castaldo

OTHER BOOKS FROM WILLIAMSON PUBLISHING